DEMON DEFENSE

AND

DEMON DOUBLING

Defend With Skill and Double for Keeps

Augie Boehm

HNB Publishing • New York

Library of Congress Control Number: 2004107198

ISBN: 0-9728061-4-8

This book is printed on acid-free paper.

The publisher offers discount on this book when ordered in bulk quantities.

HNB Publishing
250 W. 78th St., #3FF
New York, NY 10024
www.hnbpub.com

Current printing (last digit):

10 9 8 7 6 5 4 3 2 1

PRINTED IN THE UNITED STATES OF AMERICA

Preface

Since this is a bridge book, let's get right to it. You hold:

♠J32 ♡J963 ◇AQ104 ♣J6

With opponents vulnerable, partner opens 1♣, right-hand opponent (RHO) intervenes with 1♠, you double (negative), and LHO raises to 2♠. Partner jumps to 4♡, RHO persists to 4♠. What's your call?

The world champion who faced this decision passed. His partner bid on to 5♣, which could only be made with an inspired guess. Doubling 4♠, followed by killing defense, the underpinning to doubling, would have netted plus 1100! (Details overleaf.)

This is not to take a potshot at a world-class player. Bridge is an *enormously* challenging game, and everyone makes mistakes (even though a stubborn few never admit them). **Knowing when to double for penalties can swing more points in your direction than any other part of the game.** Some benefits are obvious, such as plus 1100 on this deal, but others are intangible. If you become known as a Demon Doubler, most opponents pull in their bidding horns a notch, recognizing that you are quick to wield the ax. Wary opponents are much easier to play against than aggressive bidders who constantly confront you with problems.

Doubling for penalties increases the stakes and raises the blood pressure. For this you need confidence, and that is where tight defense plays a crucial role. Good defenders are willing to risk more penalty doubles. Demon Doublers are not born; they rise from the ranks of Demon Defenders. That is why this book begins with defense, to build a confident foundation for doubling. A sound bidding style also helps: it inspires confidence to know that partner has his bids.

This is not a book for beginners; I assume you know your basics about leads and signals. It teaches you how to *use* defensive information. The Socratic method (constant questioning) that I use promotes logical thinking in a way that promulgating rules cannot.

By the end of Part I, as a graduate Demon Defender, you should be primed for the adventurous world of penalty doubles. Part II explains when to double (and when not to) and shows how defending doubled contracts, especially partials, has a rhythm of its own. When you have absorbed the lessons in this book, be prepared for a change in your bridge life. You will win more—a lot more.

Much of this material, in abbreviated form, appeared in the *ACBL Bridge Bulletin*. My thanks to eagle-eyed readers and editors who spotted some analytical errors, which I hope I have corrected.

Augie Boehm
New York City
May, 2004

Here is the full deal (from the Spingold finals), where you held: ♠J32   ♡J963   ◊AQ104   ♣J6.

E-W vulnerable   *North* (Dealer)
                           ♠ 75
                           ♡ AK82
                           ◊ 6
                           ♣ AKQ983

    West   *East*
    ♠ K96   ♠ AQ1084
    ♡ Q1054   ♡ 7
    ◊ 732   ◊ KJ985
    ♣ 1075   ♣ 42

                           South (You)
                           ♠ J32
                           ♡ J963
                           ◊ AQ104
                           ♣ J6

The bidding: *North*   *East*   *South*   *West*
               1♣   1♠   Dbl.   2♠
               4♡   4♠   ?

Let's analyze. Partner has shown a strong hand by jumping to game—your negative double didn't promise more than about six points. East's bold vulnerable 4♠ bid into the teeth of a strong auction must be based on exciting distribution, such as a two-suited hand. His second suit is odds-on to be diamonds, which you have throttled, sitting behind him. Defending 4♠ is a sure plus score, and perhaps a large one. It's time to double.

On this deal, declarer can be held to six tricks, plus 1100. Even if the defenders slip, they collect 800 against a problematic non-vulnerable game. (5♣ requires declarer to take two heart finesses through West, rather than cash top hearts. 5♡ is down if the defense leads three rounds of spades, shortening the strong trump hand.)

Contents

Preface   3

Part I: Demon Defense   9

  1. The Right Attitude   11
  2. Defend With Finesse   15
  3. A Covering Note   19
  4. Preserve Long-Suit Entry   23
  5. Hold That Entry!   28
  6. Second Hand High   33
  7. Declarer's Advantage   38
  8. Sink the Suit   43
  9. Discards   47
10. Creative Discarding   52
11. Suit Preference   57
12. Subtle Help   63

13. Patience   68
14. Quiet or Busy?   73
15. Separating Signals   78
16. Midterm Exam   84

Part II: Demon Doublinh   93

17. Penalty Doubles: The Foundation   95
18. The Timid Doubler   101
19. The Tepid Doubler: Part I   105
20. The Tepid Doubler: Part II   110
21. The Confident Doubler: Part I   114
22. The Confident Doubler: Part II   118
23. The Confident Doubler: Part III   123
24. Confidence Shaken   129
25. Confidence Shaky   133
26. Restoring Confidence   138
27. Confidence Regained   142
28. Trump Control   147
29. Going for the Kill   152
30. Partnering a Demon Doubler   157
31. Sally Fourth, Demon Doubler   163
32. Final Exam   168

PART I
DEMON DEFENSE

You have enrolled in bridge school. You are about to share the luxury of a one-on-one tutorial with a bright, intermediate-level student, Sally Fourth. The challenge of the semester is how to become a good defender, the hardest part of the game. Class by class, your instructor, the Professor, tries to lead you to think productively.

There is a set of defensive signals to provide structure, but the only set rule is to count and think. As you experience Sally's progress, you will see that hers is not a straight, upward climb. The journey is punctuated with fits and starts and moments of discouragement. There are obstacles to overcome, but Sally and the Professor share something of utmost importance—the drive to improve.

As you become involved, you, too, will improve.

1

The Right Attitude

SALLY: I think defense is dullsville. I like points, lots of points.

PROF: My dear, your rubber bridge underpinnings are showing. If you played duplicate, your tune would change.

SALLY: I don't much care for duplicate. It takes too long, people play too slowly.

PROF: Duplicate players are more deliberate because every trick of every hand might be important. Most find it challenging and stimulating.

SALLY: Where's the fun defending tiny partials? I'd as soon concede them and move on to the exciting stuff.

PROF: (*This is going to be a tough case. But there is something about her spunk....*) Sally, how often are you declarer?

SALLY: Plenty often. I bid 'em up and try to play the spots off.

PROF: No doubt, but the average player defends twice as often she declares. It's statistical: on every deal there are two defenders and one declarer; thus, you rate to defend twice as often as you declare. You'll find that it pays to study defense, and the game becomes more interesting.

SALLY: Keep talking.

PROF: You'll start to enjoy bad cards—

SALLY: Whoa, baby; not at rubber bridge.

PROF: At duplicate you can win with bad cards. The idea is to lose less than your competitors, and stonewall defense is one of the chief ways. When I played bridge at Columbia, I met a hugely talented Texan named John Bromberg. If our college teammates let a contract slip through on defense, Bromberg would drawl, "If you boys were defendin' the Alamo, Santa Anna wouldn'ta lost a single Mexican." Sally, give me a few sessions with you. I'll turn you into an eager defender, and that's a large step toward becoming a demon defender.

SALLY: I warn you, it may be uphill all the way.

PROF: We'll see. You sit East in the following deal:

North (Dummy)
♠ 63
♡ AK106
◇ 107
♣ QJ1064

East (You)
♠ QJ1092
♡ 8
◇ KJ63
♣ A72

South opens 1NT (15-17)—do you intervene, neither vulnerable?

SALLY: I was absent the day they doled out caution—I bid 2♠.

PROF: With that suit quality, OK. North bids 3♣, alerted as Stayman without a spade stopper, and South concludes with 3NT. You lead the ♠Q, partner contributes the seven, standard signals, declarer the ace. Next, declarer puts the ♣K on the table. Plan the defense.

SALLY: This must be a trick hand because I'd grab that king and fire back a high spade. Partner signaled with the seven; maybe we can run the suit.

PROF: The seven is an attitude signal, but is it encouraging?

SALLY: I know to look beneath partner's spot: the four and five are missing. Of course, half the time my partners forget to signal. That's another reason I prefer declarer play—no partner to screw things up.

PROF: I agree that it's frustrating to defend with an inattentive partner. However, a good partner makes defense a pleasure—the whole session is apt to be one big, encouraging attitude signal. Back to this deal: there is no rush to run spades, assuming that's possible. Isn't declarer likely to continue clubs if you duck your ace?

SALLY: I suppose so.

PROF: He must need to develop the suit, so you can hold your ace back until the third round.

SALLY: So what? I can't keep declarer off dummy because of the heart entries.

PROF: The idea isn't to disrupt declarer's communications; it's about learning what suit to continue. Partner may be short enough in clubs to signal revealingly. On this deal, if you hold up the ♣A, partner discards the ◊9 on the third round of clubs.

SALLY: Then I switch to a low diamond.

PROF: And you defeat the contract. Here's the full deal:

North (Dummy)
♠ 63
♡ AK106
◊ 107
♣ QJ1064

East (You)
♠ QJ1092
♡ 8
◊ KJ63
♣ A72

West
♠ 87
♡ 95432
◊ A952
♣ 85

South
♠ AK54
♡ QJ7
◊ Q84
♣ K93

Without the diamond shift, declarer wins the race, scoring two spades, four hearts, and four clubs for an overtrick. With the shift, and continuation, the contract is down one.

SALLY: Was partner's ♠7 correct at trick one?

PROF: Yes. This situation calls for attitude, and shortness in notrump is a liability, not an asset. Undoubtedly, partner was worried that the seven-spot might be misinterpreted as encouraging.

SALLY: As it was.

PROF: Waiting for a helpful discard resolved any ambiguity. *Patience* is particularly important for defense. When you declare, all 26 cards at your disposal are instantly in view. The defenders only gradually learn something of each others' holding, most often through signals that begin with the opening lead.

SALLY: Suppose West was dealt three small clubs. Is there any way he could encourage a diamond shift?

PROF: Great question. Let's say West started with ♣853. Normally, he signals count, low-high showing an odd number, when an opponent attacks the suit. However, in this situation, count is immaterial because holding back an ace can't damage declarer's communications. **Defensive principle: when attitude or count are irrelevant (or have already been signaled), the signal sent is suit preference.** If West plays his lowest club at each opportunity, he is trying to draw your attention to the lower rank-

> **J**unior high student
>
> Defenders have very few opportunities to send messages. Each message must represent valuable, new information. No room for redundancy allowed in this condensed language.
>
> **J**unior high student

ing suit, diamonds, rather than spades, the logical alternative. On the actual layout, an alert partner ought to play the ♣5, then the eight to try to convey the same message in case you held doubleton ace and were unable to see a discard.

SALLY: Well, that's pretty cool. Maybe I'm going to like defense, after all.

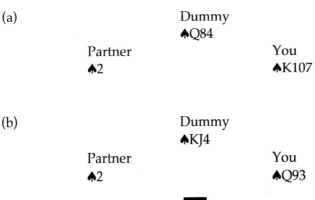

2
Defend With Finesse

PROF: Sally, at the great risk of boring you with card combinations, I must make sure that basic principles are in place. In each of the following problems, assume that you are sitting in third seat defending a heart contract. Partner leads a fourth-best deuce of spades, dummy follows with the four-spot. In each case, what card do you play?

(a)   Dummy
                                    ♠Q84
            Partner   You
            ♠2   ♠K107

(b)   Dummy
                                    ♠KJ4
            Partner   You
            ♠2   ♠Q93

(c)   Dummy
                             ♠A104
          Partner   You
          ♠2   ♠J85

SALLY: Aren't all of these finessing positions? My instinct is to play my middle card, although in (c) it feels strange.

PROF: Splendid instincts. Presuming partner didn't underlead an ace at trick one, declarer is marked with the ♠A in both (a) and (b). It is a waste to play your honor, third hand. In (c) you presume that declarer has at least one honor—partner didn't underlead KQ. It is best to save your jack to cover dummy's ten, just as you saved your king to cover dummy's queen in (a), or your queen to cover dummy's jack (b).

SALLY: Glad to hear it. In (c), what do I gain from playing my eight?

PROF: If declarer holds KQx or K9x, he is due to win three tricks, in the latter case by finessing dummy's ten after you play your jack. Even so, withholding your jack prevents dummy's ten from becoming an extra entry. If declarer has a weaker holding, like Kxx, Qxx, or Q9x, saving your jack saves a trick because you can later beat dummy's ten.

SALLY: When I hold a middle honor covering dummy's middle honor, I play third hand middle when dummy plays low.

PROF: You could put it that way. In effect, you don't play your covering honor until dummy releases its middle honor. Try another combination, again assuming hearts are trump. This time, partner leads the ♠9, traditional leads.

(d)   Dummy
                             ♠75
          Partner   You
          ♠9   ♠K862

What card do you play at trick one?

SALLY: You're trying to trick me, but I'm not biting. I play low.

PROF: Good. Why?

SALLY: Partner is leading from nothing; Q109 leads the 10 in my book.

PROF: Yes. For once, the traditional method, top from interior sequences, leaves a clearer impression than Journalist, where the nine-spot could indicate zero or two higher honors. But continue.

SALLY: Declarer must hold ♠AQJ10(x). If I put up my king, I give him the whole suit. I believe in generosity, but not at the table. Let's make this declarer work.

PROF: Exactly. Even if he uses a dummy entry to take a second spade finesse, your protected king stands in his way. He may be able to drop it on the fourth round by ruffing, but you have limited his discard potential.

Here's one more test. This time, spades are trump.

(e)   Dummy
                               ♠754

               Partner   You
               ♠8   ♠K63

How do you handle trick one?

SALLY: Hey, Prof, I'm not falling for this one either. I duck for all the same reasons.

PROF: I'm glad you understand that third hand doesn't automatically play high. When partner has lead from shortness, or top of nothing, there is nothing in his hand for you to promote. In these situations, or finessing positions, hang on to your high card.

There are a few more third-hand positions that I want to show you. Can you stand it?

SALLY: I can if you can.

(f)   Dummy
                               ◇85

               Partner   You
               ◇3   ◇AQ7

PROF: In (f) you are defending notrump on an auction that suggests partner holds a weak hand, perhaps 5 high-card points

(HCP), or less. Partner leads the diamond three, dummy follows, and it is up to you.

SALLY: I don't see the problem; the ace looks obvious.

PROF: Best third-hand play is the queen. If partner holds the king, you will continue ace and low to unblock, nothing lost. The gain comes when declarer holds Kxx(x) and partner is entryless. When you play your queen at trick one, declarer will generally release his king on the first round, fearing the ace on his left.

> Junior high student
>
> Did you know that when third hand plays high, you should follow with the lowest of equals? Third hand, from J-10-x play the ten. The play of the jack denies the ten.
>
> Junior high student

SALLY: Because if he ducks in that hypothetical layout, the defense runs the suit.

PROF: Exactly. Now, if third hand erroneously plays the ace at trick one, declarer has an easy holdup until the third round, cutting defensive communications. Does this type of thinking help you with the next problem where you are defending a club contract?

(g)
                        Dummy
                        ◊742

Partner
                                             You
◊3
                                           ◊KJ6

SALLY: I don't see any connection with the holdup concept. I know declarer has the ◊A—he can safely hold up no matter which honor I play.

PROF: Instead, consider the concept of "discovery." How might you discover the location of the missing high diamond honors?

SALLY: I already know where the ace is. If I play my king, I'm none the wiser. What happens if I play the jack? When declarer wins the ace, or holds back, I discover that partner has the queen. Aha! If, instead, my jack loses to the queen, I know that declarer has another diamond stopper. I've never made this kind of play before, but, starting now, I'm there.

3
A Covering Note

SALLY: Rules, rules, rules, I get so sick of rules. Cover an honor with an honor, second hand low, third hand high—it could drive a person crazy.

PROF: Sally, I agree that playing by rote can't compare to the stimulation of creative thinking. We've studied situations where third hand should not play high, so let's tackle second-hand defense.

SALLY: Does this mean more card combinations?

PROF: Just a few.

SALLY: Oh Prof, when do we get to real hands?

PROF: Do you like puzzles?

SALLY: Yes—why?

PROF: That's what card combinations are, mini-puzzles. Much successful defense is based on understanding everyday card positions. For instance, when you cover an honor with an honor, do you know the reason why?

SALLY: Something about promotion.

PROF: Indeed. Check yourself:

(a)   *North* (Dummy)
                                        AQ94
                 West (You)
                 K103
                                        South (Declarer)
                                        J

(b)   *North* (Dummy)
                                        AQ52
                 West (You)
                 K63
                                        South (Declarer)
                                        J

As West, do you cover declarer's jack in both situations?

SALLY: I do. In (a) I might promote my own ten, in (b) I might promote a spot for partner.

PROF: That's right. You sacrifice your honor for a purpose. In the next example, you are East and dummy's queen is led. Do you cover?

(c)   *North* (Dummy)
                                        QJ5
                                                East (You)
                                                K62

SALLY: Isn't there another rule here: cover the last of equals?

PROF: Exactly, and it's one of the best rules since there are few exceptions. You duck the queen but cover the jack on the next round. The idea is to protect partner's holding of 10xx(x) from a second round finesse in case declarer holds A98(x). Or, you can present declarer with a guess when partner holds precisely 10x, giving declarer A98xx. If you cover the first time, declarer can't go wrong. If you correctly duck, declarer may call for dummy's five-spot on the second round, misguessing that you were dealt Kx and partner 10xx. It's an old chestnut to file away for future use.

Try another.

(d) North (Dummy)
♠ Q752

East (You)
♠ KJ3

Spades are trump—South opened 1♠ playing five-card majors. The ♠Q is led from the dummy—the defenders have no ruffing potential. Do you cover?

SALLY: Seems automatic.

PROF: A reflex play, but it's wrong to cover. Picture partner's trump holding.

SALLY: Singleton or void since declarer is marked with at least five.

PROF: Right. If void, it is immaterial whether or not you cover, assuming declarer's queen play indicates an intent to finesse. You win one trick, either the second round with the jack, or the third round with the king.

SALLY: OK.

PROF: Same argument applies if partner has a singleton, *unless* the singleton happens to be the ace. Then, ducking gains a trick, not to mention escaping partner's glare when your king and his ace crash.

SALLY: Glare, sarcasm, the works.

PROF: Try one more position. Here, you are defending notrump, and, in each case, declarer calls for dummy's queen. When do you cover?

(e) North (Dummy)
Qx

East (You)
Kx

(f)   *North* (Dummy)
                                 Qx
                                             East (You)
                                             Kxx

(g)   *North* (Dummy)
                                 Qx
                                             East (You)
                                             Kxxx

SALLY: This time, I'm on my guard. I cover in (e), I cover in (f), with (g) I'm not certain.

PROF: You are trying to be selective, not play by rote. In a vacuum, covering is correct in (e) and in (f), hoping for a promotable value in partner's hand. As a general rule, **the shorter your own holding, the more length with partner, and the likelier a promotion.** When you have length (4+), the scale tilts the other way, and in (g) you can safeguard your king by ducking. Give declarer AJ109x to prove the point.

SALLY: Fair enough, but why did you refer to a vacuum?

PROF: Thus far, we have assumed that there were no special defensive considerations about the full deal. Next session, I promise you full deals that may challenge that assumption. Meanwhile, I hope we are resolved that "second hand low, third hand high," while useful enough defensive guidelines, are a poor substitute for thinking about the complete layout of the played suit.

4

Preserve Long-Suit Entry

PROF: Sally, you are almost ready for the plunge. You've solidified your understanding of common card positions for the defense. Next, let's establish some agreements about signals. What are you comfortable playing?

SALLY: As you might expect, I'm a traditionalist—fourth best, top of a sequence, ace from ace-king-x, standard attitude and count. Maybe you think that's hopelessly old fashioned.

PROF: It will do nicely. When a problem arises that would be easier to solve with more detailed agreements, I'll make a recommendation. Meanwhile, I am much more interested in your thinking than your methods.

SALLY: OK, show me some deals.

PROF: Fine—you are West in the following diagram.

North (Dummy)
♠ Q963
♡ A5
◊ 843
♣ KQ105

West (Sally)
♠ A4
♡ Q10843
◊ 107
♣ 7642

Neither vulnerable, the bidding:

North	East	South	West
P	P	1NT	P
2♣	P	2◊	P
3NT	P	P	P

South's 1NT was 15–17. You lead the ♡4. Dummy ducks, partner plays the jack, declarer the six. Partner returns the ♡7: nine, three, and ace. At trick three a low spade is led from dummy to declarer's king. What's your play?

SALLY: I think I win my ace, but let me think about it.

PROF: Too late, I'm afraid. Best defense is to duck the spade in tempo without revealing that you hold the ace. At least you considered ducking.

SALLY: No fair, Prof. You didn't say the clock was ticking.

PROF: Sally, at the table, does a bell ring when you are required to duck smoothly? You have to set your own alarm. Now, don't sulk—there's a valuable lesson in this deal. Track the hearts, the key suit for the defense.

SALLY: I haven't seen the ♡K, a critical card.

PROF: But you can deduce its location. Review trick one— partner played the jack.

SALLY: I guess you're saying that partner denied the king; in this position, third hand plays high.

PROF: Right.

SALLY: All right, declarer still has a heart stopper. Should I be switching suits?

PROF: Where, and why?

SALLY: You've got me so rattled. I don't know, just to try something new. Could partner hold a hidden running diamond suit?

PROF: A fair question—let's count declarer's HCP. In spades, he has the king and perhaps the jack; in hearts, the king for a maximum of seven HCP, thus far. Even if declarer holds both missing club honors, that only gives him 12 HCP. To make up his 1NT opening he needs at least three HCP in diamonds. We conclude that declarer has diamonds stopped.

SALLY: What's this "we?" You did all the reasoning.

PROF: Just to show you how it's done. From now on, you try to fill in the puzzle's blanks.

SALLY: Wait a minute—couldn't declarer hold queen-jack doubleton in diamonds. That satisfies the three-point requirement, yet we can still run diamonds.

PROF: Excellent point, Sally. Now, here's the objection. Your diamond construction gives partner ◊AK10xxx, yet he passed in second seat instead of opening 2◊. That's possible; we know from their Stayman sequence that partner has four spades, so a disciplined partner might well pass in second seat. The most convincing inference is that partner would have tried to cash diamonds at trick two (from AK10xxx) instead of returning a heart, and declarer wouldn't have ducked the opening lead in the first place if wide open in diamonds.

SALLY: Oh, brother. Just how is a person supposed to figure all this stuff out without putting the whole table to sleep?

PROF: The first time you try it, the process is lengthy. The next time is a little shorter, and so forth. You have to work on your performance away from the table, the way an actor studies a part or a musician a piece. That is, if you want to become good. If you're content to remain a card pusher, why bother with lessons? [*For once, Sally has no snappy retort. She broods, a bit sullen.*]

PROF: Sometimes, there is an intuitive way to find the answer. On this deal, you led hearts because you hoped to establish and cash the suit. That suggests entries are vital, doesn't it. Think like a declarer—you know to keep entries to the hand with the length. Same principle on defense—hold on to your critical entry, here, the ♠A.

SALLY: Okay, but won't declarer simply continue spades if I duck, driving out my entry?

PROF: Not necessarily. It's time for the full deal:

> *North* (Dummy)
> ♠ Q963
> ♡ A5
> ◊ 843
> ♣ KQ105

West (You)		*East*
♠ A4		♠ 8752
♡ Q10843		♡ J72
◊ 107		◊ QJ65
♣ 7642		♣ A9

> *South*
> ♠ KJ10
> ♡ K96
> ◊ AK92
> ♣ J83

Note declarer's problem. He needs five black suit tricks; his concern is that you started with more than four hearts. If you hold both black aces, or neither, the order in which he attacks the black suits is immaterial. Do you see why?

SALLY: If I have both aces, he can't shut out my hearts. If I have neither, I'm entryless, so I'm no threat.

PROF: Good. On the actual layout, repeated spade plays make 3NT. However, if the E-W aces were switched, declarer must shift from spades to clubs to attack your possible club entry. Essentially, declarer must guess which black ace you were dealt. That is why tempo and concealment becomes a factor.

SALLY: I'm beginning to get the drift. If I take too long to duck the ♠K, school's out. If I duck quickly, declarer will probably switch to clubs—at least, that's what I would do in his position. After all, how many defenders are capable of this silky smooth duck?

PROF: Not many, I grant you, but why not try to join their ranks? If you spot the *idea*—the battle to maintain entry to his long suit—you have a decent chance to prepare yourself to duck.

SALLY: Prof, don't you think you are asking too much?

PROF: From the average student, yes. From someone of your talent, no.

A student

Against an expert East, declarer should continue spades, landing the contract. If expert East held the ♠A without the ♣A, he should rise on the first spade lead to return hearts, preserving West's entry. By this reasoning, if East didn't play the ♠A, he hasn't got it.

A student

5

Hold That Entry!

PROF: Sally, do you remember my original proposal? I was to turn you into that rather rare player who loves the challenges of defense.

SALLY: Sure, I remember. I like a challenge, but I have to feel that I have some shot at success.

PROF: Let me show you one more deal. It contains an idea you have encountered before, but if the idea doesn't register, or the whole business has become too frustrating, we can call the project off.

SALLY: Show me the deal and don't worry about the health of the project or the patient. I feel I've turned a corner.

PROF: So glad to hear it. Okay, you are West in the following diagram:

North (Dummy)
♠ A64
♡ A87
◊ Q6
♣ K9632

West (You)
♠ 1073
♡ J3
◊ K9852
♣ A105

IMP scoring, both vulnerable, the bidding:

South	West	North	East
1NT	P	3NT	P
P	P		

1NT is 12–14. Naturally, you lead a fourth-best diamond. Dummy plays the queen, partner follows with the jack, declarer low.

SALLY: Wait a moment—what's the story behind partner's jack?

PROF: Right time for the question; work through the puzzle.

SALLY: If partner's jack is singleton, we're never going to establish diamonds or beat 3NT. Let's assume it's a signal.

PROF: Count or attitude?

SALLY: I'm used to attitude at trick one.

PROF: So am I; I believe that's generally more useful.

SALLY: Then partner has the ◊10 to back up the jack, meaning declarer is left with only one diamond stopper. I'm trying to track this darn suit, just like you showed me.

PROF: You're right on target. Next, declarer calls for a low club from dummy. Partner follows with the eight, declarer the queen, and—

SALLY: I'm ready. Boy, am I ready! I duck. No declarer is going to part me from my only entry.

PROF: Excellent. Declarer returns a low club.

SALLY: I duck again on general principles although, frankly, I don't see where all this is leading.

PROF: Time for the full deal:

                          North (Dummy)
                          ♠ A64
                          ♡ A87
                          ◊ Q6
                          ♣ K9632

West (You)   *East*
♠ 1073   ♠ Q952
♡ J3   ♡ Q1094
◊ K9852   ◊ J103
♣ A105   ♣ J8

                          South (Declarer)
                          ♠ KJ8
                          ♡ K652
                          ◊ A74
                          ♣ Q74

Focus on the clubs. From declarer's point of view, when you smoothly duck the first club, your original holding could have been ♣J105, leaving East with ♣A8. In that case, declarer had better duck the second club, dropping East's bare ace and depriving you of a late club entry. Of course, you must manage to duck in tempo to confront declarer with a guess.

SALLY: I understand. If declarer misguesses on the second round of clubs and ducks my ten, partner wins his jack and fires back the ◊10. Let declarer hold up his ace until the third round; he still can't use the clubs and I don't think he can make the hand without them.

PROF: Exactly. If declarer plays a third club, the defense cashes three diamonds and two clubs. Without clubs, declarer can muster only three spade tricks, two hearts, two diamonds, and one club. Either way, down one. What is the outcome if you win the first club?

SALLY: I safely continue a low diamond, thanks to partner's jack, signaling the top of a sequence.

PROF: Or, to be picky, the king with partner unblocking the jack, just in case East started with ◊J10 doubleton.

SALLY: Hadn't thought of that. In any event, declarer should hold back his ace to run partner out of diamonds. Then, declarer can safely duck the second club around to partner's jack—I never get the lead.

PROF: And declarer makes 3NT, scoring three clubs, two diamonds, two hearts, and at least two spade tricks. You recognized the main *idea*—cling to the only entry to your long suit. Brava!

SALLY: [*blushing a little*] Well, thanks.

PROF: Now, for completeness, suppose the diamonds had originally been:

North (Dummy)
◊ J6

West (You)
◊ AQ8532

Versus notrump, you lead your five-spot and dummy's jack wins the trick. How should partner signal?

SALLY: Don't we show attitude at trick one?

PROF: Yes, but here it is sensible to signal count when third hand can't top dummy's card of jack or lower. Like standard count signals, East's low-high sequence shows an odd number; with an even number he begins a high-low. To see how this may be helpful, let us assume that you (West) gain the lead in a suit outside diamonds. Should you now plunk down the ◊A, trying to drop a bare king in the closed hand, or should you shift, lest you establish declarer's king?

SALLY: I would know if I could tell how many diamonds declarer held. You're saying I can tell, based on partner's count signal.

PROF: Yes. Suppose partner played the four?

SALLY: That's his lowest, showing an odd number, hopefully three, not one. Then, declarer started with Kx and I can run my suit, ace first.

PROF: Right, and what if partner signaled with the ten?

SALLY: Partner started with a doubleton, declarer with Kxx—I won't continue diamonds.

PROF: Only under special circumstances, such as cashing out to save an overtrick.

SALLY: I'm beginning to appreciate why good defense is sexy. It's a twosome working in close communication.

[*The Professor was content.*]

6

Second Hand High

SALLY FORTH: One of the things I like about defense is that it makes me visualize the unseen hands. This must be helpful in any phase of the game.

PROF: Is that ever true! A beginner's focus is on his own 13 cards; the intermediate player absorbs partner's messages, building it into a 26-card game. The budding expert must play the 52-card game. For instance, here is a simple illustration.

North (Dummy)
◊ KQJ10

East (You)
◊ A72

Defending notrump against an entryless dummy, you duck when the ◊K is led from dummy, declarer playing the four-spot, partner the eight. Next, declarer calls for dummy's ◊Q—how do you handle your ace?

SALLY: I need to calculate how many diamonds declarer holds. To do that, I have to figure out how many diamonds partner has.

PROF: Exactly.

SALLY: Partner is trying to help me by signaling count. Using standard signals and assuming his eight is the beginning of a high-low, he is telling me he started with an even number of diamonds, two or four. If it is two, declarer has four and I can't break his communications. If partner has four, leaving declarer with two, I should win my ace on the second round.

PROF: Yes, limiting him to one diamond trick.

SALLY: That wasn't too hard.

PROF: Fair enough, but the thought process was valuable. You had to count the diamond suit, visualize the different layouts, then determine which play was the most effective. Let me show you a more complete defensive problem.

North (Dummy)
♠ AQ
♡ J109874
♢ 732
♣ 86

East (Sally)
♠ 852
♡ A2
♢ 10865
♣ K932

The bidding:

South	North
2♣	2♠ (Alert)
2NT	3♢ (Transfer)
3♡	4♡
6NT!	P

A word about the auction: North's 2♠ response showed two controls, an ace or two kings, creating a game force. This helps explain South's unusual sequence. 2NT was evidently a temporizing move, because if South held the customary 22–24 points, he would presumably pass the 4♡ signoff. Instead, South must hold extra values—picture a big, balanced hand.

SALLY: OK, what's the opening lead?

PROF: Partner leads the ♠4, fourth best. When dummy is displayed, what strikes you?

SALLY: The long heart suit.

PROF: Good, and, since you hold the ♡A, you may be able to play a key role in this deal. Declarer wins the ♠Q, you follow with the deuce, declarer the six. At trick two, declarer advances dummy's ♡J—what do you do?

SALLY: On general principles I duck fast. Maybe partner has the queen.

PROF: Let's try counting, that great unraveller of bridge mysteries. Between your hand and dummy, you can account for 14 HCP. If partner has the ♡Q, that leaves declarer with a maximum of 24 HCP. I'm just subtracting 16 HCP from the 40 in the deck.

SALLY : I'm not as fast, but now I'm with you.

PROF: We concluded that declarer needs more than 24 HCP to justify his leap to 6NT. He didn't ask for aces or use Roman Keycard Blackwood to check on heart quality. If South is trustworthy, and his sophisticated bidding technique suggests this to be the case, he holds all the missing high cards and partner is busted.

SALLY: OK, but what's the big deal?

PROF: Focus on the hearts, the critical feature. Is there any holding where you can cut declarer off from dummy's long suit?

SALLY: If declarer holds ♡KQx, I don't see a way, as long as he unblocks his heart honors.

PROF: Keep going.

SALLY: If declarer holds KQ tight and I duck the first round, declarer continues the suit, forcing my ace and establishing the rest while dummy still has an entry, the ♠A.

PROF: Don't stop now.

SALLY: I've got it! If I rise immediately with the ace and return a spade, I remove dummy's entry while the hearts are still blocked. Wow, it's exhausting.

PROF: Come on, Sally, you did good work. Here's the full deal:

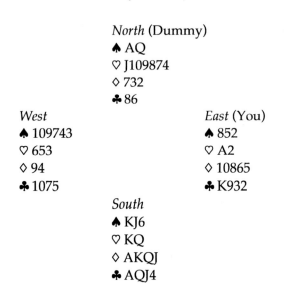

North (Dummy)
♠ AQ
♡ J109874
◊ 732
♣ 86

West
♠ 109743
♡ 653
◊ 94
♣ 1075

East (You)
♠ 852
♡ A2
◊ 10865
♣ K932

South
♠ KJ6
♡ KQ
◊ AKQJ
♣ AQJ4

When you win the first heart and return a second spade, dummy is stripped of entries and declarer is shut off from the long hearts. The best he can manage is to finesse in clubs with dummy's final entry, run his winners, and finish down two. If you duck the heart, declarer scores five hearts and seven other top winners without a finesse. Remember to compliment partner for his opening lead, prosaic though it was. Only early defensive spade plays were able to remove dummy's entries.

A student

While second hand low is usually correct, the exceptions occur on deals where entries are everything. Then, second hand high may be necessary, either to foul declarer's communications (here), or preserve a defensive link (see the A student card on p. 27).

A student

SALLY: Why did I flub that problem?

PROF: The problem was made more difficult by having to reconstruct the key suit immediately, without any defensive signals. Still, as we saw, the information was available from the auction. The rest was visualizing the blockage and acting accordingly.

SALLY: I wonder if the peculiar bidding threw me, or maybe it was that tricky jack of hearts, pretending to finesse?

PROF: Perhaps, but here's a tip. If an experienced opponent uses an unusual sequence, assume there's a logical reason. Think along with the opponent and try to find it.

7
Declarer's Advantage

SALLY: More and more I'm enjoying defense, but I think I still prefer the thrill of declaring.

PROF: No doubt about the thrill of the well-played deal—you are the featured performer. Still, we agree on the importance of becoming a good defender.

SALLY: As you say, we defend twice as many deals as we declare.

PROF: If you and partner are both quality defenders, you will often score best when the cards run against you.

SALLY: Why?

PROF: On defense you are both in play, contributing a steady stream of good, winning decisions. But when your side declares, one of the skilled players is sidelined.

SALLY: Hadn't thought of that.

PROF: Since you love to declare, let's declare even though we are studying defense. There's a clear connection between the two skills, as I hope you will see. In the diagram, assume that you are declaring 4♠ against the lead of a diamond honor.

North (Dummy)
♠ J53
♡ K87542
◊ 95
♣ 82

South (You)
♠ AKQ76
♡ A3
◊ A102
♣ J94

SALLY: I'd love to use dummy's hearts; the problem is entries. If I draw three rounds of trumps, I cut myself off from the dummy: I can establish the hearts, but I can't reach them.

PROF: Right.

SALLY: So I think I'll draw just two rounds of trump, saving dummy's jack. Assuming a 3-2 trump split, I play ace, king, and another heart, ruffing high. Assuming another 3-2 split, I cross to dummy's ♠J, pulling the trumps, and run three more hearts.

PROF: Excellent. With a good plan and friendly splits, you win 11 tricks; five spades, five of dummy's six hearts, and the ace of diamonds. Now, what would change if the defenders lead clubs, cash two rounds, and play a third?

SALLY: Let's see. I ruff in the dummy but I have a problem bringing in the hearts.

PROF: You certainly do. It is impossible to both establish hearts and completely draw all the trumps. You should abandon hearts and plan to concede a diamond, then ruff a diamond. Ten tricks is the limit.

SALLY: That third round of clubs does a job on my entries. Reducing dummy to two trumps wrecks the suit establishment plan.

PROF: Hold on to that principle. On the next deal, shift to defense.

North (Dummy)

♠ A108

♡ 98

◊ A9653

♣ K82

East (You)

♠ 974

♡ AQJ

◊ QJ2

♣ A943

Playing IMPs, both vulnerable, the opponents reach 4♠ through the following sequence:

South	*North*
2♠	2NT
3◊	3♠
4♠	P

2♠ was preemptive, 2NT asked for a feature, 3♠ was invitational. Partner leads the ♡3, fourth best. You win the ace and continue with the ♡Q, winning the trick as partner follows with the deuce. What next?

SALLY: Declarer must have six good spades and the diamond king for the feature response. I'm worried about dummy's diamonds establishing for a bunch of discards. Maybe I should cash my ♣A before I lose it. Or perhaps I should shift to a passive trump and wait.

PROF: These are general impressions; instead, try to develop a clear picture of the deal. Declarer is likely to hold six spades for the weak two, three little hearts since partner has indicated king-fifth, and the ◊K for his feature response. If declarer has three or more diamonds, you can afford to wait for a diamond and a club trick.

SALLY: Wait; what if declarer's singleton club is the queen? Won't he build a discard for the third diamond?

PROF: Yes, he will, and since there's nothing you can do to prevent it, forget about it. The danger is that declare holds Kx in diamonds and, thanks to the 3-3 split, dummy's diamonds will furnish two discards.

SALLY: That's what I said, and that's why I want to cash out and save the overtrick.

PROF: There's a better way. Observe the effect of a third round of hearts, forcing dummy to ruff, in the following layout.

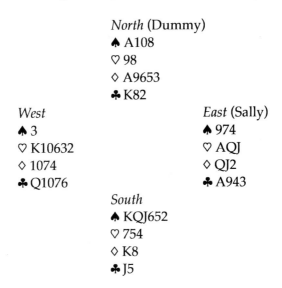

North (Dummy)
♠ A108
♡ 98
◊ A9653
♣ K82

West
♠ 3
♡ K10632
◊ 1074
♣ Q1076

East (Sally)
♠ 974
♡ AQJ
◊ QJ2
♣ A943

South
♠ KQJ652
♡ 754
◊ K8
♣ J5

SALLY: Oh, no—I can't believe it! It's the same story as the previous deal. When I punch dummy down to two trumps with the third round of hearts, declarer can't ruff out the diamonds and draw trumps except by finishing in his hand. Then, he must lead clubs and our side wins two club tricks, setting the contract.

PROF: Exactly. Shifting to a trump allows declarer to ruff out the diamonds and draw trumps, finishing in the dummy. The two discards produce ten tricks: six spades and four diamonds. Cashing the ♣A prematurely yields the same result.

SALLY: Why didn't I see it coming? I recognized the idea as declarer.

PROF: Indeed you did. Declarer's advantage is that the 26 cards you will use are laid out before you. A defender must con-

K een-eyed declarer

South could make 4♠ against
best defense by ruffing the third
round of diamonds after taking
the heart ruff in dummy. Then, a
spade to dummy's ten and play
an established diamond winner.
If East discards, discard a club
loser. If East ruffs, overruff and
finish trumps in the dummy,
cashing the last diamond for a
club discard. However, this line
fails when trumps are 2-2 or 3-1
with the length in West and the
♣A onside.

K een-eyed declarer

struct partner's hand, usually only in part, with clues from the bidding or early defense. Obviously, that's a much harder task. The
same principles of card play apply equally to declarer or the defenders. Card positions are mathematical, or geometrical, so the
principles that govern them tend to be universal. What works for
offense works for defense, and vice-versa.

SALLY: It's what I've heard you say: first, get the picture, then
try to use the information. Boy, it makes me mad when I flub it.

PROF: Hang in there, Sally. A strong defender is a rare breed,
and she is not created overnight.

8
Sink the Suit

SALLY: I enjoyed what we did last lesson, taking first the offensive, then defensive view of a similar card position.

PROF: Glad to hear it. A clear defensive perspective is often difficult to obtain, but, once in place, is subject to universal card play principles. For example, assume you are declaring 3NT against the lead of the ♠3, fourth best.

North (Dummy)
♠ 105
♡ 64
◊ A9
♣ KQJ7542

South
♠ QJ2
♡ AKQ3
◊ Q752
♣ 108

East wins the spade ace—what's your plan?

SALLY: Simple—develop the clubs, using the ◊A for entry.

PROF: Any risks?

SALLY: If spades are skewed and the ♣A is with the spade length, I'm toast. However, the lead means the spades are 4-4, unless the opening leader is being cute.

PROF: So is the contract safe, assuming an orthodox lead?

SALLY: It seems that way.

PROF: What if the defense shifts to diamonds before you are able to attack clubs?

SALLY: Ah, I see your point. If they drive out dummy's diamond ace early, the club suit is finished.

PROF: Correct, barring a lucky singleton ace of clubs, preventing a defensive holdup.

SALLY: Anything I can do, or does it depend on the defenders?

PROF: Good question. You would like to influence the defenders to continue spades—try dropping the queen at trick one. Do you see why?

SALLY: To make it look like I was dealt Q-J alone. If the defenders think they can run spades, they won't consider diamonds.

PROF: That is the illusion you hope to create. Indeed, East is apt to continue spades at trick two—hiding your deuce makes it possible that West led from a five-card suit. When you follow with the deuce on the second round, West may credit East with an original spade holding of AJxxx. At any rate, by falsecarding in spades you hope to avoid the devastating shift to the ◊K! Even if declarer ducks, a diamond continuation strips dummy of its priceless entry.

SALLY: Haven't I seen that spectacular play somewhere?

PROF: It has a name, the Merrimac Coup, the sacrifice of a high honor to sink a long suit. It's a striking application of an ordinary defensive idea—attack entries to the long suit. Now, shift gears and sit East—you are defending 3NT at IMPs.

> The *Merrimac* was an American cargo ship that was deliberately sunk in Santiago Harbor in 1898 to impede the Spanish fleet during the Spanish-American War.

North (Dummy)
♠ AQ
♡ 32
◊ QJ10932
♣ J86

East (You)
♠ J643
♡ A1094
◊ AK
♣ Q109

South opens a 15-17 1NT, North raises to 3NT. West leads the ♡5, fourth best. You win the ♡A, declarer follows low. Plan your defense.

SALLY: I can account for all the hearts under the five, so partner has led from a four-card suit, not longer.

PROF: Where are the missing HCP?

SALLY: I count 14 in my hand and 10 in dummy. Subtracting 24 from the 40 in the deck, declarer has them all for his 1NT, or partner has a measly jack.

PROF: Good, keep going.

SALLY: It seems natural to return a heart to hammer that suit home.

PROF: You are playing IMPs—will you defeat the contract?

SALLY: Assuming declarer develops diamonds, we win the ♡A, two top diamonds, and the fourth round of hearts. Perhaps I'll get a late club.

PROF: This deal is typical of the *race* at 3NT—will declarer win nine tricks before the defense wins five? To help you analyze, here is the complete deal:

North (Dummy)
♠ AQ
♡ 32
◊ QJ10932
♣ J86

West
♠ 1087
♡ J865
◊ 764
♣ 732

East (You)
♠ J643
♡ A1094
◊ AK
♣ Q109

South
♠ K952
♡ KQ7
◊ 85
♣ AK54

SALLY: I see that heart continuations don't work. Declarer sets up dummy's diamonds, pitching his losing black cards.

PROF: Correct. Is there any way sink dummy's diamonds?

SALLY: I've got it! At trick two, return a spade. When I regain the lead in diamonds, pound another spade. There goes dummy's A-Q of spades, there go the diamonds, there goes the contract.

PROF: Exactly.

SALLY: Darn, why didn't I see the move before viewing the deal diagram?

PROF: It's the difficult, but necessary, step of visualizing, then reacting. A shortcut might help: when an opponent holds a long suit with tenuous entries, it is often a winning idea to attack the entries.

SALLY: You make it sound easy, but it's not.

PROF: As declarers, we know the importance of preserving long suit entries. The defensive side of the coin is to remove them. If this deal occurred at matchpoint scoring, it would be pure guesswork. If declarer has a tripleton diamond, the spade shifts are ineffective because there is a late diamond entry. A spade shift allows an expensive overtrick, while heart continuations hold declarer to his contract.

9

Discards

SALLY: Want to know what's difficult for me? Discarding, especially when declarer runs a long suit.

PROF: Join the club, Sally; it's difficult for us all. Just to agree on basics, you use traditional carding methods, right?

SALLY: Attitude signals at trick one and first discard, high card encourages. Count signals when an opponent initiates a suit, high-low to show an even number. Standard suit preference signals. Should I be doing something else?

PROF: There is definite merit in upside-down attitude signals, saving high spot cards when you hold trick-taking potential. Odd-even at the first discard—odd numbered cards encourage, even cards discourage and indicate suit preference—is also popular among experienced partnerships. The information is more detailed, but declarer may benefit more than the defense. More than any method, bridge reasoning and counting are the biggest assets.

SALLY: The signals I play are habits of a lifetime. I think it's less disruptive if I stick to traditional methods and develop my reasoning.

PROF: Fine with me. Now, before we discuss your particular question of discarding, let's cover a few general situations. Sitting East, you hold: ♠1082 ♡AQ109 ◊64 ♣8752. South opens 1NT (15–17), North raises to 3NT. Partner leads the ◊10 and this is what you see:

North (Dummy)
♠ K43
♡ KJ
◊ AJ32
♣ J1094

East (You)
♠ 1082
♡ AQ109
◊ 64
♣ 8752

You follow with the four, negative attitude. Do not routinely echo with a low doubleton defending notrump; shortness is no asset. Declarer wins the king in hand and runs three more diamonds, partner starting with 10-9-8-7. You have two discards to make—what shall they be?

SALLY: If partner gains the lead, I'm dying for a heart shift, but if I discard a high heart spot I'm tossing away a trick. If I throw the deuce of spades and the deuce of clubs, maybe partner will get the message by default.

PROF: Well done; here's the full deal:

North (Dummy)
♠ K43
♡ KJ
♢ AJ32
♣ J1094

West
♠ J975
♡ 853
♢ 10987
♣ K6

East (You)
♠ 1082
♡ AQ109
♢ 64
♣ 8752

South
♠ AQ6
♡ 7642
♢ KQ5
♣ AQ3

Eventually, declarer will finesse in clubs, losing to partner's king. For lack of anything better, partner should find the heart shift for down one. Note that declarer might have done better to win the opening lead in dummy and take an immediate club finesse. Partner's job is much tougher with no helpful discards to guide him. Try another. As East, playing matchpoints, you hold:
♠10   ♡QJ62 ♢J852   ♣7432.

South opens 1♠, North offers a game-forcing raise, and South settles for 4♠. Partner tables the ◊K, revealing:

North (Dummy)
♠ KJ75
♡ 87
♢ 1064
♣ AKQ6

East (You)
♠ 10
♡ QJ62
♢ J852
♣ 7432

First, what are your lead conventions?

SALLY: I like ace from A-K (x), king from K-Q (x).

PROF: OK, how do you signal at trick one?

SALLY: I play partner for the ♢Q, so my jack makes me encourage.

PROF: Be precise; which spot card?

SALLY: What a nag—I play my eight.

PROF: Thank you. More importantly, your partner will thank you for making matters clear. Declarer ducks the first diamond. Partner, confident that you hold the jack, continues the ♢Q. Declarer wins the ace and peels off five rounds of trump; partner follows twice, then discards the ♡5. What are your four discards?

SALLY: Hmm. A low diamond is easy, so is one low heart. I hate to unguard my heart combination; therefore, I'll ditch a couple of small clubs.

PROF: Pity. Here's what I mean:

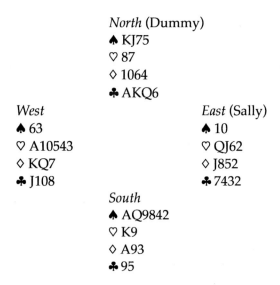

North (Dummy)
♠ KJ75
♡ 87
♢ 1064
♣ AKQ6

West
♠ 63
♡ A10543
♢ KQ7
♣ J108

East (Sally)
♠ 10
♡ QJ62
♢ J852
♣ 7432

South
♠ AQ9842
♡ K9
♢ A93
♣ 95

Dummy's ♣6 scores an expensive overtrick. This can be prevented if you hold all your clubs and release three hearts. Usually, declarer will cash dummy's top clubs, throwing a diamond, and play towards his ♡K, making four when the finesse fails. If, instead, declarer cashes his final trump, you must let go of your last heart honor, just to guard clubs and diamonds.

SALLY: I see it in the diagram, but how can I get it right at the table?

PROF: **Keep equal length with an opponents' side suit if you hold a stopper.** Here, you are the only defender who can cover dummy's little club, so your lowly ♣7 is elevated to stopper status, just like your ◊J. You protect clubs and diamonds, partner guards hearts—his high ♡5 (the three and four are missing) promises an honor. That is the general way defenders try to survive pressure discards—early signals indicating how they will divide responsibilities.

10

Creative Discarding

PROF: Dialing direct is the clearest way to communicate, but sometimes a defender's message must be sent indirectly. Let's say you want to encourage suit A but you don't have a readable card to play, or the signal card may represent a trick. Instead, you may have to signal negatively in suits B and C. Partner will wind up playing suit A, which is what you want.

SALLY: Please show me an example—you're starting to sound inscrutable.

PROF: It must be the Chinese lunch. Sit East in the following diagram:

North (Dummy)
♠ Q743
♡ J74
♢ Q4
♣ K972

East (You)
♠ 96
♡ 85
♢ 1097652
♣ A106

The bidding:

South	West	North	East
1♠	2♡	2♠	P
4♠	P	P	P

Partner leads ace, king, and queen of hearts—what do you discard at trick three?

SALLY: I'm itching to throw the ten of clubs but it can't hurt to think it through. If partner's ♡Q holds, it would be nice to beat this contract fast. However, declarer may be ready to ruff. If so, have I given away anything important?

PROF: Keep going.

SALLY: Sometimes a ten helps take a trick. I guess I could get my club message across by discarding the deuce of diamonds. If partner holds the lead, he will shift to a club by default.

PROF: The diamond deuce is best; while the ♣10 is fatal. Check the deal diagram:

North (Dummy)
♠ Q743
♡ J74
♦ Q4
♣ K972

West   *East* (You)
♠ 82   ♠ 96
♡ AKQ1032   ♡ 85
♦ 83   ♦ 1097652
♣ J53   ♣ A106

South
♠ AKJ105
♡ 96
♦ AKJ
♣ Q84

If you reduce to doubleton ace of clubs, declarer can draw trumps and lead a low club from dummy. You duck, declarer wins the queen and ducks a club on the way back. Two natural defensive club tricks condense into one, contract makes.

SALLY: I had a suspicion that the ♣10 was valuable.

PROF: Indeed. Note that if partner had won trick three, there was no urgency to grab the setting trick. Declarer won't have enough discards. In fact, if declarer started with

♠ AK10xxx   ♡xxx   ♦AK   ♣Jx

the defenders must *avoid* leading clubs, or else they jeopardize the two defensive club tricks they have been dealt.

The next problem requires a deft touch. You are East, defending 4♡, and partner leads the ♠K.

North (Dummy)
♠ 632
♡ J96
◊ AKQ4
♣ K43

East (You)
♠ A4
♡ Q3
◊ 107652
♣ QJ102

SALLY: Any bidding clues?

PROF: South opened 1♡ and rebid 2♡ over a 2◊ response—North drove to game. How do you handle trick one?

SALLY: I know this one, Prof. I overtake partner's spade and play one back, unblocking and preparing for a ruff.

PROF: Good. At trick two, declarer follows with the nine, partner wins the ten. Partner continues with the ♠Q—pick your discard.

SALLY: I've seen this too; pitch the ♣Q to show a sequence.

PROF: That's an appropriate maneuver, but for a different occasion. Let's focus on how we might obtain the setting trick. Not diamonds and not clubs; declarer is marked with the ace.

SALLY: Why?

PROF: Where are his HCP? He opened the bidding without the A-K-Q of spades or diamonds, and you are staring at the Q-J in hearts and clubs.

SALLY: All right, he has at least the A-K of hearts and the ♣A. My queen of hearts will drop.

PROF: Yes, but it represents your only chance for an extra trick. The full spade position isn't proven, but try to visualize the possibilities.

SALLY: I guess declarer must follow to the third spade for us to have a chance. If spades are distributed 5-3-2-3 starting clockwise with West, I give up.

PROF: Right, so keep thinking.

SALLY: If spades are 4-3-2-4, I see a hope—I can score my trump queen on an overruff.

PROF: Excellent, so now the problem is clear: how to induce partner to play a fourth round of spades in the following diagram:

North (Dummy)
♠ 632
♡ J96
◊ AKQ4
♣ K43

West   *East* (You)
♠ KQ108   ♠ A4
♡ 84   ♡ Q3
◊ J983   ◊ 107652
♣ 876   ♣ QJ102

South
♠ J975
♡ AK10752
◊ Void
♣ A95

SALLY: Isn't a spade continuation natural? He has a count on the spades.

PROF: Yes, but he isn't certain that you can beat dummy's ♡J. From partner's position, South's opening could include the A-K-Q sixth of hearts and the black jacks. Then, a club switch to your hypothetical A-Q is necessary before dummy's diamonds provide crucial discards.

SALLY: OK, I'm with you, but how can I signal my trump honor?

PROF: Not directly, but you can discourage partner from switching to clubs, the logical alternative. Then, he will play the fourth spade by default.

SALLY: Beautiful! I discard the ♣2, preventing the club shift. Dummy makes it obvious to avoid diamonds, so partner will back into the winning spade continuation. What did you call it? A deft touch?

PROF: Sometimes in bridge dialogues, a hint is as helpful as a holler.

11

Suit Preference

PROF: The defenders' most frequent and useful signals are attitude and count. Suit preference is number three on the short list, but it is often vital.

SALLY: I recognize suit preference when giving a ruff. If I lead a high spot, I want a shift to the higher ranking side suit (excluding trumps); a low spot asks for the lower ranking.

PROF: Yes, and it can be useful at trick one, defending a trump contract, when dummy shows a singleton in leader's suit.

SALLY: Sometimes it's tricky to know which of the three signals applies.

PROF: A governing principle can help here: when attitude and count are already known, either from previous signals or the bidding, or are *immaterial*, then suit preference applies. Let's practice—you sit West:

North (Dummy)
♠ 742
♡ K83
◊ 95
♣ KQJ102

West (You)
♠ K103
♡ 107642
◊ K863
♣ A

Both vulnerable, South opens a 15–17 1NT. The vulnerability persuades you to pass, and North raises to 3NT. You lead a fourth-best heart, dummy follows with the three and partner the five, declarer winning the queen. At trick two, a low club is led; you win as partner contributes the nine. How do you defend from here?

SALLY: Hearts are hopeless if partner can't do better than the five spot.

PROF: Agreed, but might you continue anyway, merely to be passive?

SALLY: I hadn't gotten that far, but I suppose I could. A shift could blow a trick, hitting an ace-queen combination in the closed hand. Frankly, I'm guessing and I hate to guess.

PROF: So do I, but here we have a clue—consider partner's club nine.

SALLY: Isn't it the beginning of a high-low, signaling an even number of clubs?

PROF: On this deal is count important?

SALLY: I guess not.

PROF: Surely not, since dummy has a guaranteed entry. Since club attitude and count are immaterial, this becomes a suit preference situation.

SALLY: In that case, partner's high club indicates a preference for spades, the higher ranking of the two candidates.

PROF: Exactly. Consult the deal diagram:

North (Dummy)
♠ 742
♡ K83
◇ 95
♣ KQJ102

West (You)
♠ K103
♡ 107642
◇ K863
♣ A

East
♠ AJ865
♡ 5
◇ 10742
♣ 953

South
♠ Q9
♡ AQJ9
◇ AQJ
♣ 8764

SALLY: That's neat. I shift to a spade and we run the suit, down two. Any other shift allows the contract to make.

PROF: Correct, and a diamond shift concedes an overtrick. Partner's thoughtful carding paved the way.

SALLY: Provided that it was understood.

PROF: Isn't that the essence of partnership? Try another. You hold: ♠7 ♡AK10854 ◇98 ♣9862. As dealer, favorably vulnerable, you open 2♡, LHO doubles, partner leaps to 4♡, and RHO chimes in with 4♠. You pass and LHO raises the ante to 6♠, ending the auction. You lead a high heart, preferably the king, and dummy tables:

North (Dummy)
♠ AK4
♡ J
♦ K652
♣ AKQJ4

West (You)
♠ 7
♡ AK10854
♦ 98
♣ 9862

Partner follows with the seven, declarer the six. What do you make of the situation?

SALLY: First off, why did I lead the king when we play ace from ace-king combinations?

PROF: Against a slam, it is better to let the king lead generate a count signal, often solving a cashout problem. The ace lead, common versus a slam, denies the king and requests attitude.

SALLY: Always something to learn. Anyway, I interpret partner's seven as suit preference since dummy holds a singleton in my suit. Who cares about count here.

PROF: Good. So, assuming traditional methods, what is partner's message?

SALLY: The seven-spot is hard to read. If the seven is high, partner wants a diamond shift. If it's his lowest heart, the seven asks for a club. Both look plausible: partner might hold the ♦A or a club void.

PROF: Indeed. What does it mean if partner's seven is a middle spot?

SALLY: It must mean he has no preference.

PROF: Therefore, it denies the ♦A or a club void because he could have asked for those shifts, yet he didn't. OK, it's time to unmask that seven-spot: is it high, low, or middle?

SALLY: Partner has at least four hearts for his bid. Examining the spots, the queen and nine are the only missing higher hearts. If the seven is his lowest, that gives partner Q-9-7, a three-card preemptive raise. Impossible.

PROF: Could the seven be his highest spot? Look underneath the seven.

SALLY: Okay, let's see. Declarer played the six, so only the three and two are missing. Partner wouldn't jump on 7-3-2. If it's not his highest or lowest, it's a middle-sized heart.

PROF: Good spot work.

SALLY: I'm exhausted—can I go home?

PROF: Sally, like many tasks, the first few times are the most difficult. Then, it starts to get easier. How do you use the information you've so laboriously acquired?

SALLY: I'm not sure; lead a trump?

PROF: No—continue a high heart. Here's why:

A student

This suit preference signal works best when the signaler has at least three-card length, so that a high, low, and middle signal are all available.

West (You)
♠ 7
♡ AK10854
♢ 98
♣ 9862

North (Dummy)
♠ AK4
♡ J
♢ K652
♣ AKQJ4

East
♠ J863
♡ Q973
♢ J1073
♣ 3

South
♠ Q10952
♡ 62
♢ AQ4
♣ 1075

When dummy ruffs, partner's jack of spades is promoted. On any other continuation, declarer plays ace-king of trumps, picks up partner's jack with a proven finesse, and claims. Put yourself in partner's place at trick one. He sees that a heart continuation will remove dummy's small trump, preventing a late finesse. He tries to discourage a specific shift by playing a middle heart. The rest is up to you. Your singleton trump might create a suspicion that partner has length. In any event, you abandon other lines of defense and play for the trump promotion by default.

SALLY: I thought a singleton in dummy demanded a shift, but I can see that is wrong.

PROF: A dummy singleton makes a continuation unlikely, not impossible. When third hand needs a continuation, a middle card, to avoid emphasizing a shift, is the ticket.

12

Subtle Help

PROF: Sally, I have a really challenging deal for you. It would be wasted on someone less talented and motivated.

SALLY: Thanks for the compliments, Prof; I accept the challenge.

PROF: Good. You hold: ♠KJ863 ♡QJ5 ◇K1093 ♣9. Match-points, neither vulnerable, RHO opens 1♣ and you overcall 1♠. LHO bids 1NT, partner passes, and RHO closes it out with 3NT. Partner tables the ♠5, dummy reveals:

North (Dummy)
♠ 97
♡ A82
◊ Q8
♣ AKQJ72

East (You)
♠ KJ863
♡ QJ5
◊ K1093
♣ 9

Dummy plays low. First decision: which spade do you play at trick one?

SALLY: Reading those darn spots, partner's lead could be either top of a doubleton (the four and two are missing), a singleton, I suppose, or low from length. In case it's the latter, I'll try the king.

PROF: Yes, partner could hold ♠A105. In fact, declarer wins the ace. Does that clarify the spade position?

SALLY: I don't see how.

PROF: It likely places the queen,

SALLY: Let me try to reconstruct your reasoning. If partner led from Qxx, declarer with Axx would hold back the ace.

PROF: Good deduction, and there is an additional spade clue from the auction. South's voluntary 1NT call shows values, roughly 7–10 HCP. Counting visible HCP and subtracting from 40 leaves partner with 4–7 HCP. If partner held a spade fit, he might well have raised to 2♠. His likeliest spade holding is shortness.

SALLY: I like the way you reason.

PROF: Declarer, who started with a doubleton club, now runs dummy's six-card suit. In the blind, how would you discard?

SALLY: A low spade is painless; the rest looks like torture. I don't want to unguard any suit.

PROF: Placing declarer with A-Q of spades limits him to about four HCP elsewhere. It would be most helpful to know the location of the missing honors.

SALLY: Sure would, but it seems like guesswork. The 1NT call doesn't guarantee solid stoppers except in spades.

PROF: True, so we need input from partner.

SALLY: But I have to commit to early discards while he follows suit four times.

PROF: Therefore, *how* he follows suit must provide a clue—that is the need for the defense.

SALLY: Wouldn't a count signal usually apply?

PROF: Club count is irrelevant. Remember the general principle? When count and attitude are known or immaterial, suit preference operates. If partner plays his lowest club at each juncture (up the line), he is showing strength in diamonds, the lower of the two unplayed suits. A succession of high clubs (down the line) promises heart strength. Mixing it up shows no preference, or, by agreement, strength in the original suit, spades.

SALLY: That's neat.

PROF: It is sensible because it transmits a useful message at no cost. Now, back to this deal. Partner's first club is the eight spot, then the six, four, and three. What are your conclusions?

SALLY: Partner is signaling like crazy that he likes hearts, so he must have the king. Therefore, it seems that I can toss my hearts and guard diamonds and spades.

PROF: Excellent. This is the end position:

North (Dummy)
♠ 9
♡ A82
♢ Q8
♣ Void

          East (You)
          ♠ J86
          ♡ Void
          ♢ K109
          ♣ Void

SALLY: By the way, what did partner discard on the last two clubs?

PROF: Alert question; the ♠4 and ♡3.

SALLY: Confirming an original doubleton spade.

PROF: Right. Declarer, meanwhile, threw two small hearts,

then two small diamonds. In the end position the ♡A is cashed—what's your discard?

SALLY: Declarer and I currently hold the same spade length, so I better hold my spades to keep parity. Bye-bye, diamond nine, nice knowing you.

PROF: Good counting, good choice. Declarer follows with a low heart and advances dummy's ♠9—do you cover or duck?

SALLY: I duck fast.

PROF: Declarer lets it ride—the finesse is virtually guaranteed—and leads the ♢8 to his ace. He then continues diamonds, tossing you on lead. Endplayed, you must return a spade into his Q-10, making six. Re-examine the six-card ending, played cards in parentheses.

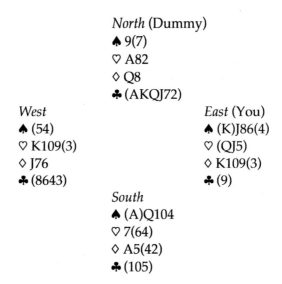

North (Dummy)
♠ 9(7)
♡ A82
♢ Q8
♣ (AKQJ72)

West
♠ (54)
♡ K109(3)
♢ J76
♣ (8643)

East (You)
♠ (K)J86(4)
♡ (QJ5)
♢ K109(3)
♣ (9)

South
♠ (A)Q104
♡ 7(64)
♢ A5(42)
♣ (105)

Do you see how to avoid the endplay?

SALLY: I do now. Cover the nine of spades when it is led. Then, my spade spots stand up for a trick at the finish. Gosh, that's a tough hand to defend.

PROF: It is indeed, but if you do everything right, you hold declarer to eleven tricks. That earns you a fine score because there are so many opportunities for error. The keys are to interpret partner's suit preference club plays, retain spade parity with the closed hand, and track the spade spots all the way. You may have forgotten the spade seven, played from dummy at trick one. That empowered your ♠86 in the ending.

SALLY: I did forget, but I enjoyed that deal, even if I wasn't perfect. I guess I like the challenges of defense.

PROF: You didn't use to say that.

13

Patience

SALLY: Now that I have all these signals and strategies floating around in my brain, I find I'm more confused than ever. I never seem to know whether I should be shifting, signaling, underleading, or whatever.

PROF: First of all, temporary confusion is normal when you are acquiring new knowledge. It takes time for the new to settle in, to be synthesized. Second, why must you be *doing* anything? Some defenses are best conducted by doing nothing. Observe:

North (Dummy)
♠ AQJ
♡ J5
◊ KQ3
♣ A8753

East (You)
♠ K102
♡ 9
◊ J108542
♣ J109

The bidding (neither vulnerable):

West	North	East	South
3♡	Dbl.	P	4♠
P	P	P	

Partner cashes two top hearts while you discard a small diamond. Partner continues the ♡Q, declarer ruffs with the ♠J. Your move.

SALLY: I'm thinking of overruffing and returning a diamond. Maybe partner is void.

PROF: What sort of preempt does that give partner?

SALLY: Seven hearts to the A-K-Q, plus a void. I see; too strong for a 3♡ opening, not vulnerable. Okay, after I overruff, I'll shift to clubs. Can't hurt, might help.

PROF: What will you accomplish? At best, partner will hold the ♣Q; any slow club trick can wait.

SALLY: I guess there's no rush. Ah, of course! Don't overruff at all. Then, I must score two trump tricks, my king and the ten, promoted out of thin air. Why didn't I see that?

PROF: Like most defenders, you're forever looking to be active. On this deal, there was no reason to grab the lead. When you hold a sure trump trick in an overruff position, it's usually best to wait. Try another problem.

North (Dummy)
♠ 84
♡ AQ7
◇ 10862
♣ KJ85

West (You)
♠ A93
♡ 108652
◇ 7
♣ 9643

The bidding (both vulnerable):

East	South	West	North
1◇	1♠	P	1NT
2◇	2♠	P	P
3◇	3♠	P	P
P			

Partner wins your opening diamond lead with the jack and cashes the ace, declarer following. Partner continues the ◇Q, declarer ruffs with the ♠Q. How do you defend?

SALLY: My normal reaction is to overruff and then think, but this time I'll think first.

First, has partner given me a suit preference indication? I know he started with the four top diamonds. At trick three, he still held the K-Q—he chose the queen. Does that signal interest in the lower ranking side suit, clubs?

PROF: If partner has the ♣AQ, is that consistent with the bidding? You must go backwards before you know how to go forwards.

SALLY: Slave driver. All right, if partner held the ♣AQ in addition to his six solid diamonds, he probably would have bid more at his second turn. Is that what you're looking for?

PROF: Keep probing. Declarer seems to have seven spades for his auction; why didn't he preempt?

SALLY: Good question. My guess is that he has too many high cards outside spades.

Okay, I'll give him the ♡K and ♣Q. But wait. If I don't shift to a club pronto, declarer may take a quick discard with the high hearts.

PROF: Don't panic. Test the hypothesis by counting declarer's distribution. He is known to hold two diamonds and, presumably, seven spades. If his hearts are Kx, and his clubs Qx, one discard can't help him.

SALLY: All right, you've worn me down. I surrender—I'm too tired to make any plays.

PROF: Sally, since we have finally determined that there is nothing urgent to do, do nothing. Instead of overruffing, discard. Declarer crosses to dummy's ♡Q and leads a spade to his king, partner following low.

SALLY: Now I take my ace and shift to a club.

PROF: Good. Check the deal diagram:

```
                    North (Dummy)
                    ♠ 84
                    ♡ AQ7
                    ◇ 10862
                    ♣ KJ85
West (You)                          East
♠ A93                               ♠ 5
♡ 108652                            ♡ J43
◇ 7                                 ◇ AKQJ54
♣ 9643                              ♣ A72
                    South
                    ♠ KQJ10762
                    ♡ K9
                    ◇ 93
                    ♣ Q10
```

Partner wins the ace of clubs and shoots back a fourth diamond. Declarer cannot shut out your trump nine, the setting trick. Notice that the trump promotion campaign fails if you overruff immediately. Try it. The key is to begin weakening declarer's trumps while your trump holding remains intact.

SALLY: That was a lot of effort to promote a nine-spot.

PROF: Perhaps. This kind of race goes to the patient, not the swift.

A student

Note that declarer crossed to dummy to lead the first round of trumps. This was careful play, hoping for singleton ace with East. If South could have retained all his trump honors, he would have averted the trump promotion.

student

14

Quiet or Busy?

PROF: One of my mentors, the late Edgar Kaplan, used to lecture at New York's Card School, in its day a unique institution. It occupied a swank address, catered to the carriage trade, and sported a faculty that read like a *Who's Who* in the world of bridge.

He was fond of the next deal, and it speaks directly to our discussion of active versus passive defense. You are West:

North (Dummy)
♠ A93
♡ A74
◊ K743
♣ AQ2

West (You)
♠ Q842
♡ KQ10
◊ QJ10
♣ J84

The bidding:

North	*East*	*South*	*West*
1◊	P	1♡	P
1NT	P	2♡	P
P	P		

North's 1NT rebid shows 15–17. N-S are playing the weak notrump, a cornerstone of the Kaplan–Sheinwold system. You lead the ◊Q; it holds. You continue the ◊J, declarer ruffs. Declarer continues with a low trump, allowing your ten to hold, partner following. Plan the defense.

SALLY: I play a heart honor.

PROF: Declarer wins dummy's ace, ruffs a diamond, and exits in hearts. You have reached the following position:

North (Dummy)
♠ A93
♡ Void
♢ K
♣ AQ2

West (You)
♠ Q842
♡ Void
♢ Void
♣ J84

East
♠1065
♡Void
♢A
♣ K97

South
♠ KJ7
♡ J
♢ Void
♣ 1053

You are endplayed. Let's say you try a low club. Declarer ducks in dummy, East wins. East must be careful to return a club. If he shifts to a low spade, declarer ducks in hand and the defensive spade trick goes up in smoke. On this deal, both sides battle to avoid breaking a fresh suit. In the black suits, whichever side breaks the suit loses a trick.

SALLY: That nine of spades and ten of clubs sure are powerful. How does one recognize such situations?

PROF: The best indicator is the sight of the dummy. Some dummies are threatening to the defense, some aren't, and it has nothing to do with HCP. This dummy was non-threatening. There was no ruffing power to neutralize. There was no long suit that might establish to generate useful discards. This means that the defenders must pursue a passive course. Try not to break fresh suits; instead, return suits that have already been played.

SALLY: That's what declarer and I were doing in the red suits, going back and forth.

PROF: And in the seven-card ending, East does best to stick with clubs, rather than branch out into spades. It's one of the most difficult lessons to teach because defenders are forever thrashing

about, hoping to "find" partner. It is a sign of bridge evolution
when the defender realizes that less may be more. Now, for contrast:

                        North (Dummy)
                        ♠ A64
                        ♡ A832
                        ◊ 73
                        ♣ J973
                                              East (You)
                                              ♠ 5
                                              ♡ KQ10
                                              ◊ AKJ105
                                              ♣ KQ102

The bidding (E-W vulnerable):

East	*South*	*North*	*West*
1◊	3♠	P	4♠
Dbl.	P	P	P

SALLY: Is East's double for penalties?

PROF: Not purely. N-S have announced a big spade fit. East,
under the gun, is doubling more on high cards than trump tricks.
4NT was available for takeout on a highly distributional hand.
West leads the ◊Q. Before you plan the defense, ask yourself
whether this is a menacing dummy.

SALLY: There's no long suit to worry over, but maybe the diamond shortness is a threat. What do I know about the diamond position? Did partner lead the queen because it's the highest card in
my suit?

PROF: That's very outdated, and for good reason. Partner
leads an honor either because it is top of a sequence, or from shortness. Here, you can tell which it is.

SALLY: Sure, it's shortness because I'm looking at the jack.
OK, partner has one or two diamonds. That gives declarer five or
four. Now, I sense the menace. Dummy's doubleton diamond is in

the perfect place for declarer. If we don't prevent it, declarer will trump his losing diamonds in dummy.

PROF: You had best prevent it.

SALLY: Of course. Overtake the diamond and shift to a trump.

PROF: Excellent. Let's say declarer wins in his hand and advances the diamond nine, partner following with the eight.

SALLY: I'm on lead again, this time without a trump. I need to find a way to get partner on lead. A club seems the only possibility.

PROF: Yes, and to ensure success, shift to a low club so that partner must win the trick. (Hopefully, declarer is not void.) Partner has a spade to return, and we nip the contract by one trick. Consult the deal diagram:

North (Dummy)
♠ A64
♡ A832
♢ 73
♣ J973

West
♠ 82
♡ J9765
♢ Q8
♣ A864

East (You)
♠ 5
♡ KQ10
♢ AKJ105
♣ KQ102

South
♠ KQJ10973
♡ 4
♢ 9642
♣ 5

Look at all the work you had to do to hold declarer to nine tricks. Diagnose the lead, note the ruffing threat, overtake to direct the defense, and underlead your club sequence, late in the day, to prevent partner from making a mistake by ducking.

SALLY: That's what I call an active defense.

PROF: You are approaching the status of Demon Defender.

15

Separating Signals

PROF: I have a nice illustration of the logic and language of defense to show you.

SALLY: Which comes first, logic or language?

PROF: Logic. Defensive language serves the logic—by signaling, we arrange to send the messages that the logic of the situation requires.

SALLY: Sounds very professorial. Could I see an example?

PROF: Of course. You pick up:

♠Q1073   ♡K6   ◊Q105   ♣QJ42

RHO opens 2NT (20–21), LHO bids 3◊ (transfer), RHO completes the transfer with 3♡, and LHO raises to 4♡. You table the ♣Q and dummy greets you with:

North (Dummy)
♠ 854
♡ QJ982
◇ K873
♣ 7

West (You)
♠ Q1073
♡ K6
◇ Q105
♣ QJ42

At trick one, partner plays the 10 as declarer wins the ace. Declarer cashes the ace of trumps and continues with the five-spot, partner following with the three and four .You are on lead; what do you do next?

SALLY: First, I need to make sense of partner's ♣10 at trick one. Clearly, it's a signal, but it's not clear to me *what* is being signaled.

PROF: Fair enough, but don't proceed without trying to form a conclusion.

SALLY: OK. When dummy shows a singleton in a suit contract, it is normal for the signal to be suit preference. If that's the case, partner is screeching for a spade shift. However, something troubles me. North's bidding is unusual—he insisted on hearts, even though it might be only a 5-2 fit.

PROF: Astute perception. Does partner's carding in trumps tell us anything?

SALLY: Partner played up the line, showing an even number of hearts. By the way, why is trump count opposite from count in the other suits?

PROF: So that partner can save a potentially useful high trump spot when commencing a doubleton signal. Back to this deal, did partner start with two hearts or four?

SALLY: I'd say four because declarer would have tried a heart finesse if he held A10xx and partner held a doubleton.

PROF: Excellent. Now, how does all this speak to partner's high club at trick one?

SALLY: Frankly, I wish I knew.

PROF: You're so close to the answer, don't stop now. Here's a hint: since partner holds four hearts, a forcing defense is a logical option.

SALLY: All right, that makes sense, and dummy has the master trumps that might need to be shortened.

PROF: Yes.

SALLY: Therefore, if partner took that overview when dummy appeared, he should be helping me find the pump suit.

PROF: Exactly the need for the defense on this deal.

SALLY: Then, partner's ♣10 is an attitude signal, and I should continue a club at trick four.

PROF: Congratulations! You seal declarer's fate since this is the complete layout:

North (Dummy)
♠ 854
♡ QJ982
♢ K873
♣ 7

West (You)
♠ Q1073
♡ K6
♢ Q105
♣ QJ42

East
♠ 96
♡ 10743
♢ J9
♣ K10953

South (Declarer)
♠ AKJ2
♡ A5
♢ A642
♣ A86

When you continue clubs, dummy will ruff, reducing to partner's trump length. Let's say declarer tests a third round of trumps, hoping for a 3-3 split. If he finishes drawing trump, you discard a spade. The best declarer can do is cash his winners for down one. If he tries for an endplay, or finesses in spades, your club exit allows partner to cash three club tricks, down two.

SALLY: What happens if declarer takes a spade finesse right now?

PROF: You continue the forcing game with another club. It does declarer no good to refuse the force; partner overtakes with the ♣K and continues the suit. All roads at this point lead to down two as the defense has gained control.

SALLY: What a difference if I misinterpret partner's ♣10 as suit preference. Our defense collapses.

PROF: It certainly does. A spade shift not only concedes a trick to the ♠J, but grants declarer time to draw trump and establish dummy's fourth diamond. The result is an overtrick instead of an undertrick.

SALLY: Sometimes it's tricky to know which signal applies.

PROF: Since defenders have very few opportunities to send messages, the quality of the information they transmit must be of high utility. At trick one, attitude is signaled when relevant. That was the case here since the master hand appeared in dummy, which often happens in transfer sequences. When in doubt about the intent of a signal, apply this moral: **Assume that your empathetic partner has just told you what you most needed to know.**

A student

The information that defenders transmit may sometimes be of more value to declarer. It takes great skill—and another book—to weigh the tradeoffs. To illustrate the defensive quandary of whether to send a straightforward signal, or practice deception, consider the deal on p. 82. You are East.

North (Dummy)
♠ 8762
♡ J104
◇ AQ3
♣ K63

East (You)
♠ AK3
♡ 75
◇ K862
♣ J1082

South opens 1NT (15–17), North closes it out with 3NT. West leads the ♠Q. To unblock, you alertly overtake the ♠K, cash the ace, and continue a third spade. Declarer follows twice, then discards the ◇7 and ◇10 as partner cashes high spades. What do you discard on the fourth round?

If you discard the ◇8, partner will indeed shift to a diamond. That's the good news. Here's the bad news—consult the deal diagram.

North (Dummy)
♠ 8762
♡ J104
◇ AQ3
♣ K63

West
♠ QJ105
♡ 9862
◇ 954
♣ 97

East (You)
♠ AK3
♡ 75
◇ K862
♣ J1082

South
♠ 94
♡ AKQ3
◇ J107
♣ AQ54

Naturally, if declarer finesses in diamonds, you score your king for down one. But declarer saw your encouraging diamond. If he takes it at face value, he should reject the doomed diamond finesse, rise ace, and run four heart tricks. Here is the position, with East still needing to find one discard.

                          North
                          ♠ Void
                          ♡ Void
                          ◊ Q
                          ♣ K63

        West   *East* (You)
        ♠ Void   ♠ Void
        ♡ Void   ♡ Void
        ◊ 95   ◊ K
        ♣ 97   ♣ J1082

                          South
                          ♠ Void
                          ♡ Void
                          ◊ Void
                          ♣ AQ54

East is squeezed. Any discard gives declarer a trick and the contract. If East sees this end position looming, he won't betray the location of the ◊K at trick five, discarding either a heart or a deceptive low diamond. Left in the dark, declarer has choices. If West shifts to a diamond at trick five, declarer may decide the try the diamond finesse, a better percentage than hoping for a 3-3 club split. If West shifts to a heart instead, declarer should defer a final decision, cashing four hearts, reducing all hands to:

                          North
                          ♠ Void
                          ♡ Void
                          ◊ AQ
                          ♣ K63

        West   *East*
        ♠ Void   ♠ Void
        ♡ Void   ♡ Void
        ◊ 954   ◊ K8
        ♣ 97   ♣ J1082

                          South
                          ♠ Void
                          ♡ Void
                          ◊ J
                          ♣ AQ54

As before, East still has to find a discard. A club is fatal, but a low diamond is not. Although East blanks the ◊K, declarer doesn't know the situation. Why shouldn't he finesse? Note that this final discard must be made smoothly. If East agonizes before unguarding his king, declarer is quite apt to reason why and play for the drop.

16

Midterm Exam

Test your third-hand play. In problems 1–4, you are East, defending a notrump contract. West's card represents partner's opening lead. North is the dummy and plays low at trick one. Which card do you play? (*Answers are on p. 89.*)

1.   *North*
                              ♠ Q84

West   *East* (You)
♠2   ♠K107

2.   *North*
                              ♠ 942

West   *East* (You)
♠J   ♠KQ1083

3.   *North*
                                 ♠ Q76
          West   *East* (You)
          ♠3   ♠A1082

4.   *North*
                                 ♠ K62
          West   *East* (You)
          ♠7   ♠AQ105

In problems 5–8, the same format applies, but you are defending a suit contract.

5.   *North*
                                 ♠ KJ4
          West   *East* (You)
          ♠2   ♠Q93

6.   *North*
                                 ♠ K103
          West   *East* (You)
          ♠2   ♠J84

7.   *North*
                                 ♠ 754
          West   *East* (You)
          ♠9   ♠K1082

8.
                                 North
                                 ♠ 754
          West   *East* (You)
          ♠3   ♠K862

Test your reactions to partner's third-hand play. In the following problems, you are West, defending 3NT. You have led fourth best, dummy (North) has followed low, East and South have played the indicated card, completing trick one. Later in the play, you regain the lead in some other suit. Do you continue the original suit (hearts) or shift? If you continue, which card?

9.

	North	
	♡ 842	
West		East (You)
♡KJ73		♡10
	South	
	♡ Q	

10.

	North	
	♡ 54	
West		East (You)
♡K1093		♡ Q
	South	
	♡ A	

11.

	North	
	♡ 54	
West		East (You)
♡Q9732		♡J
	South	
	♡ K	

12.

	North	
	♡ 54	
West		East (You)
♡Q9732		♡ 10
	South	
	♡ A	

13.

North (Dummy)
♠J2
♡7
◊AJ8763
♣5432

East (You)
♠85
♡A1095
◊KQ94
♣1076

The bidding:

South	West	North	East
1♠	P	1NT	P
3♠	P	4♠	All pass

Opening lead: ♡K. Plan your defense.

14.

North (Dummy)
♠ AK86
♡ 104
◊ AJ5
♣ QJ92

East (You)
♠ 542
♡ J987
◊ K642
♣ 83

The bidding:

South	West	North	East
1♡	P	1♠	P
2♡	P	4♡	P
P	P		

Opening lead: ♣A. Plan your defense.

15.   *North* (Dummy)
                                         ♠Q10
                                         ♡A84
                                         ◊Q8752
                                         ♣754
                    West (You)
                    ♠K83
                    ♡752
                    ◊94
                    ♣AKJ102

The bidding:

South	West	North	East
1♡	2♣	2♡	P
4♡	P	P	P

You cash the A-K of clubs. Partner follows with the 3 and 9, declarer with the 8 and Q. Your move.

16.   *North* (Dummy)
                                         ♠ A1042
                                         ♡ 109
                                         ◊ K65
                                         ♣ KQJ9
                                                     East (You)
                                                     ♠ 9
                                                     ♡ 8742
                                                     ◊ A874
                                                     ♣ A543

The bidding:

South	West	North	East
1♠	P	2NT	P
4♠	P	P	P

North's 2NT shows spade support and an opening bid. South's 4♠ shows a minimum opening and denies an outside singleton or void. West leads the ◊J (standard leads), dummy ducks. What do you play to trick one? When declarer pulls two rounds of trump, what is your first discard?

ANSWERS

If the answers are confusing, lay out the cards to help you follow the analysis.

1. Finesse your ten. You save a trick when South was dealt AJx or Axx. Against Jxx, you break even.

2. Overtake with the queen. If partner led a singleton jack (because you bid the suit), you can continue. If you duck and declarer ducks, the defense loses a valuable tempo in the race.

3. Finesse your ten. You gain a trick when South started with Kx or xx. Versus Jx, you break even.

4. Play the five! The only higher spades are the 8-9-J, and if partner led fourth best, he must have them all. Leave him on lead to run the suit. (If you bid spades, partner's lead may be from shortness. Then, winning the queen is probably best.)

5. Finesse your nine. The ace is marked with South—you save a trick when partner holds the ten.

6. Finesse your eight. When partner has led from Q9xx (South holds Axx), you save a trick. If South has A9x, you break even.

7. Play the deuce. The lead marks South with AQJ, so playing the king simply gives your opponent three fast tricks. Duck to make him use a dummy entry to take a second spade finesse. Sometimes, he doesn't have the entry, or he may need it for another purpose.

8. Play the king. At last, third-hand high. Here, you sacrifice your king to promote spade values for partner, one of the chief purposes of third-hand high.

9. Continue, and play your king. Partner's ten-spot denied the nine. If declarer started with AQ9, you are on your way to establishing your suit.

10. Shift. Declarer is marked with the ace-jack of hearts. Unless it is specifically doubleton, wait for partner to continue the suit to shut out the ♡J.

11. Shift. Declarer started with ♡AK10—partner's jack denied both the ten and the ace (third-hand high). If you continue hearts, you concede a trick to declarer's ten.

12. Continue with the deuce, showing a five-card suit. Your basis is that declarer won the king instead of a cheap trick with the jack. Unless he is playing a deep game, partner is marked with the ♡J.

13. Overtake with your ♡A and shift to a trump. This dummy contains two threats, the long diamond suit and the shortness in hearts. You have diamonds well stopped, but you need to get busy to counteract the ruffing value. A trump shift from your side is safe. Partner may be unable to see the need for a trump shift, or a trump shift may cost him a trick from holdings like ♠Kx or Qxx. South's hand: ♠AK10963 ♡J62 ◊10 ♣AKJ; West: ♠Q74 ♡KQ843 ◊52 ♣Q98. Against your trump shift, South is down one. If you defend passively, declarer scores five spades in hand, two heart ruffs, one diamond, and two clubs.

A student

In Problem 12, an expert declarer might deceptively win the king from AKJ if he desperately feared a shift to an unstopped suit. If he has made such a fine play, tip your hat and pay off.

student **A**

14. Play your ♣3, negative attitude. On this deal, you don't need a club ruff—you start with one natural trump trick; ruffing doesn't help. What you do need is a diamond shift to promote your king. The best you can do is discourage clubs—partner has to do the rest. If partner finds the diamond shift, the contract is set one. Otherwise, declarer makes game. South's hand: ♠J3 ♡AKQ652 ◊Q10 ♣1054; West: ♠Q1097 ♡3 ◊9873 ♣AK76.

15. Shift to a low spade to comply with partner's suit preference signal. Partner started with three clubs—holding a doubleton, he would have signaled high-low. He knows from your 2♣ bid that declarer can hold no more than two clubs, and he knows that you too will have the club count. He has played his highest remaining club (the nine) to help you with your shift, indicating a preference for the higher ranking suit, spades. Cash two top spades before declarer uses dummy's diamonds. South's hand: ♠J54 ♡KQJ96 ◊AKJ ♣Q8; East: ♠A9762 ♡103 ◊1063 ♣963.

16. Play your eight at trick one. If you rise ace, you give declarer two fast diamond tricks. At your first discard, make it the ♡2. Declarer will develop clubs. Win your ace and return a heart, hoping partner has a quick entry. If all goes well, partner will process the combination of your encouraging diamond and discouraging heart to return the ◊10, leading to down one when South has: ♠KQJ763 ♡KQ ◊Q32 ♣106; West: ♠85 ♡AJ653 ◊J109 ♣872.

PART II
DEMON DOUBLING

Welcome back from semester break. When you share Sally's achievement of becoming a competent, hence confident, defender, certain possibilities immediately open. You are now eager to exercise your new defensive muscles, and the most profitable way is to use the penalty double to set opponents when they overbid.

Of course, it takes nerve. If they make their doubled contract, you tend to get a very poor result. That's where confidence enters, and the better you defend, the more willing you are to "take them on." Nothing will earn you more tops than learning how to become a Demon Doubler.

In the coming semester, the Professor shows Sally what it takes to double for penalties. For instance, would you act, holding this hand, ♠A83 ♡A7 ◇AQ5 ♣KQ952, in the following auction?

You	LHO	Partner	RHO
1♣	1◇	P	1♡
Dbl.	2♡	2♠	3♡
?			

A discussion and analysis takes place during the first class of the new semester. The answer may surprise you.

17

Penalty Doubles: The Foundation

PROF: One sure sign that you're facing an expert pair is if they double you for penalties in a low part-score. Think back—when was the last time you defended or declared a doubled contract like 1♠, 2◊, or 3♣?

SALLY: I think you're right—for most of us, it hardly ever happens. Frankly, we're frightened. We're frightened they will make their contract, giving us a zero. We tend to panic and misdefend. Also, we're never sure whether partner is doubling for penalties, or takeout, or support, or general strength.

PROF: Doubtless, there are many reasons why low-level penalty doubles are rare, even for quite seasoned players. Nevertheless, I'm making it my next mission to convert you into a confident doubler. Not only will you reap matchpoint and IMP rewards, but you will become a respected, even feared, player. Opponents think twice before butting in with trash against players who know how to go for the jugular.

SALLY: You're asking a lot, Prof.

PROF: Sally, you have made a quantum leap—you've become a competent, hence confident, defender. That's a crucial prerequisite to becoming a demon doubler. You are less likely to shrink from these high-reward/high-risk situations. If you wish to be a complete player, you have to include this weapon in your arsenal. Once you become familiar with *how* to defend a doubled partial, you will be more inclined to pull the doubling trigger.

SALLY: The only thing I know about penalty doubles is that it helps to have long, strong trumps.

PROF: Good, because that's the most important component of successful doubles of low-level contracts. Other vital considerations are the position of your trumps—best when sitting behind your opponent's trumps—and the strength you can expect partner to provide. Of course, vulnerability is often a factor.

SALLY: And high-card strength.

PROF: That depends. Let's say as South you hold

♠A83   ♡A7   ◊AQ5   ♣KQ952

Neither vulnerable, matchpoints, the auction goes:

South (You)	West	North	East
1♣	1◊	P	1♡
Dbl.	2♡	2♠	3♡
?			

What's your call?

SALLY: 19 of the finest. I'm impressed; I double. I assume it's penalty.

PROF: Not purely. Your first double (takeout) announced short hearts. A second double doesn't alter that picture; it merely refines it. Here, it shows extra strength and offers partner options.

SALLY: I hope partner passes for penalties.

PROF: Don't be dumbfounded if they wrap it around your neck. You don't hold any nasty surprises for declarer. The trumps are splitting well, your ◊Q appears onside, partner is very weak.

SALLY: He volunteered 2♠.

PROF: After not being able to bid 1♠ a round earlier. Why shouldn't the deal should look like:

```
                              North
                              ♠ J6542
                              ♡ 83
                              ◊ J42
                              ♣ 764
         West (Dummy)                          East
         ♠ 103                                 ♠ KQ9
         ♡ Q542                                ♡ KJ1096
         ◊ K10983                              ◊ 76
         ♣ AJ                                  ♣ 1083
                              South (You)
                              ♠ A83
                              ♡ A7
                              ◊ AQ5
                              ♣ KQ952
```

On defense, your side wins a trick in each suit. Declarer coasts home in 3♡ doubled, plus 730. On offense, you can win only seven tricks in spades; 3♠ is minus 200.

SALLY: Hard to believe that the winning call is pass. All right, if that's not a good penalty double, what is?

PROF: I'll show you. You hold: ♠864 ♡65 ◊AQ93 ♣A962. Both vulnerable, your partner in fourth seat opens 1♡, RHO intervenes with 2◊.Assuming you play negative doubles, what's your plan?

SALLY: 2NT to show game invitational strength and general distribution. Should I be worried about the lack of a spade stopper?

PROF: Not really, but you should be concerned that you are letting RHO off the hook. All signs are promising to collect a juicy penalty.

SALLY: I just don't see it. I have 10 HCP and let's say partner holds 13. Is that enough combined strength to sock it to 'em?

PROF: Think tricks, Sally, not points. If you defend a diamond contract, your hand represents about four tricks, three diamonds and one club.

SALLY: Wait a minute—where is the third diamond trick? I

All I see is my A-Q combination sitting over the probable King.

PROF: Yes, your trump honors are well located. The third trick rates to be your nine-spot in conjunction with your heart shortness, but we'll get to that in a minute. When partner opens the bidding, credit him with a minimum of two defensive tricks.

SALLY: Sometimes I open light.

PROF: Light in HCP doesn't affect doubling, as long as an opening bidder or intervenor can deliver some tricks. 10 HCP including two aces provide a sound basis; 12 HCP in queens and jacks do not. Back to our problem: counting combined defensive tricks, we expect a minimum of six: four from us, two from partner. This calculation projects that plus 200 is available at this point in the auction. Do you know the significance of plus 200?

SALLY: Yes; if this is a partscore deal, plus 200 on defense beats any partial made on offense.

PROF: Right. Therefore, on this auction, what should our plan be?

SALLY: Okay, let's say that there's blood in the water, although I still don't smell it. You're implying that I should pass and hope that partner re-opens with a double. What if he doesn't? He doesn't know I made a trap pass.

PROF: When he is short in the opponent's suit, made more likely because of your length, he must strain to double, largely to accommodate a trap pass on your part. That's an important corollary to the negative double, catering to a potential trap pass. If partner is too distributional to defend 2◊ doubled, he bids a suit, leaving us free to explore notrump if it seems wise.

SALLY: Kind of like having two bites at the apple.

PROF: Indeed. Assume that you maneuver to defend 2◊ doubled, the full auction being:

RHO	YOU	LHO	Partner
P	P	P	1♡
2◊	P	P	Dbl.
P	P	P	

You lead the ♡6, and let me show you the full deal to help you follow the defense.

North (Dummy)
♠ KJ932
♡ J102
◊ 84
♣ Q73

West (You)   *East*
♠ 864   ♠ AQ5
♡ 65   ♡ AQ873
◊ AQ93   ◊ 52
♣ A962   ♣ 1084

South (Declarer)
♠ 107
♡ K94
◊ KJ1076
♣ KJ5

First of all, do you like your prospects?

SALLY: Off the top, we should win two spade tricks, one heart, two diamonds, and one club. Down one; close double.

PROF: Not close at all—watch. Partner wins the ♡A and returns the eight spot, suit preference for spades, right? He assumes that you led from shortness, because if you had a heart fit you would rarely convert his double. A likely misfit is a prime feature of this type of defense.

SALLY: That's useful to know.

PROF: Declarer ducks the heart return to dummy's ten and leads a trump, losing the trump finesse to your queen. You return a small spade to give count, partner wins his queen (say) and gives you your heart ruff. You continue spades to partner's ace, and he does best to persevere with a fourth round of hearts. At this point, here is the trump position:

North (Dummy)
◊ 8

West (You)   *East*

◊ A9   ◊ 5
                    South
                    ◊ KJ76

When East leads a heart—everyone else holds a heart void—South, who has no useful pitches, will probably trump with the ◊J in an attempt to shut out your trump nine. This presents you with the opportunity to make a key defensive play. Discard, don't overruff. In a twinkling, you have promoted your trump nine.

SALLY: That's neat. I remember the idea from our lessons on defense. (*See Chapter 13, Patience, p. 68.*)

PROF: Remember this technique. It occurs with particularly frequency when defending doubled small partials because that's when you are blessed with long, strong trumps which declarer can't pull quickly. If you have the patience, you will have the time to develop your trump holding to the maximum.

> **J**unior high student
>
> Successful penalty doubles are founded on accurate defense and reasonably sound requirements for opening bids— a minimum of two defensive tricks. If you favor a very aggressive bidding style, you will have to be more conservative with your doubles.
>
> Junior high student

SALLY: How many tricks did we take on defense?

PROF: We scored the ace of hearts, the ace of clubs, two top spades, and *four* trump tricks. Plus 800 on a part-score deal will IMP or matchpoint nicely.

SALLY: Okay, Prof. I'm not there yet, but you've got me thinking.

18

The Timid Doubler

PROF: The bridge player who confidently executes low-level penalty doubles is no instant pudding. What holds players back is a lack of confidence. First, the would-be defender has to know the ingredients of a successful recipe.

SALLY: I know that a strong trump holding is usually necessary, and it helps to hold shortness facing partner's length. Then, there is that matter of trump promotion that you were showing me.

PROF: Indeed. These types of defenses are imbued with a distinctive rhythm. Since declarer can't draw trumps quickly, the defenders have time on their side to establish and cash side-suit winners. Then, it is a matter of maximizing the trump potential. Patient development is often the key to success.

SALLY: I think you've identified why defenders like me have trouble. On the rare occasion when we double, we're so nervous that they might make their contract that we grab any trick we see.

PROF: That's probably true, but practice and experience

should modify that bad habit. Let's take an example. You hold:
♠7   ♡Q9743   ♢9842   ♣AJ5. Both vulnerable, partner opens 1♠
in third seat. RHO intervenes with 2♡. What do you do?

SALLY: I'm too weak for an invitational 2NT, so I pass.

PROF: Good. LHO passes, partner reopens with a double,
RHO passes, and it is back to you.

SALLY: Here we are, and I hate it. I'm tempted to bid 2NT
now, trusting that partner will draw the inference that I was too
weak to bid 2NT earlier.

PROF: Weak is what you hold—for *offense*. Where will the
tricks come from? The singleton spade augurs badly for offense,
but it is splendid for defense against 2♡—you rate to win several
ruffing tricks. Convert partner's takeout double to penalties by
passing.

SALLY: Let's say I accept what you say. However, if they
make 2♡, I have doubled them into game. What's the score, minus
670? Zeros don't come any rounder than that.

PROF: Sally, there are other aspects of the question, not nearly
so gloomy. Since the opponents are vulnerable, if you defeat them
by only one trick, you score plus 200, a likely top because that
beats any partial your side might achieve. Second, you don't have
to beat every contract you double. One of my mentors said, "If the
opponents never make a doubled contract against you, then you
aren't doubling often enough." If you score two tops to every bottom, you average about 67%, winning most duplicates hands
down. Playing IMPs, double more conservatively. The basic
change is to avoid doubling for a one-trick set.

SALLY: On your example hand, I understand that you want
me to pass and play for penalties at matchpoints. Should I take out
partner's takeout double playing IMPs?

PROF: No, because prospects are much rosier than a one-trick
set. To see why, let's defend. Naturally, you lead the ♠7, and this is
what you see:

North (Dummy)
♠ Q10953
♡ 6
◇ J10
♣ 109843

West (You)
♠ 7
♡ Q9743
◇ 9842
♣ AJ5

At trick one, partner wins the ♠A and returns the ♠6 for you to ruff, declarer following with the ♠8 and ♠K. What next?

SALLY: Partner's spade return is suit preference. It looks like his highest spade spot, so I interpret his signal as a request for diamonds, the higher of the two unplayed suits.

PROF: Good, so which diamond do you return?

SALLY: Does it matter? Since I play fourth best, I suppose I return the ◇2.

PROF: I would return the ◇9, top-of-nothing, an attitude signal. If partner realizes that you hold no diamond honors, he will look to clubs for your outside strength. Partner wins your ◇9 with his king, thinks it over, and shifts to the ♣2. Declarer produces the king, you win your ace.

SALLY: That's sweet. Since partner's ◇K won an earlier trick, I'll presume he holds the ace and continue with a diamond.

PROF: Make it the deuce to show that your current count is an odd number. Partner wins his ◇A, declarer following low, and cashes the ♣Q, everyone following. At this point, the defense has taken the first six tricks. Partner next plays a third round of spades, declarer ruffing with the ♡J. Your move.

SALLY: Oops. I was about to overruff with my ♡Q, but I don't need to since the queen is still protected. I discard.

PROF: Excellent. Declarer's current trump holding happens to be ♡AK1082, yours is ♡Q974. By discarding, you promote your trump nine into an extra winner. When the dust settles, the defense has won a total of eight tricks, setting 2♡ doubled three tricks for plus 800. Here's the full deal:

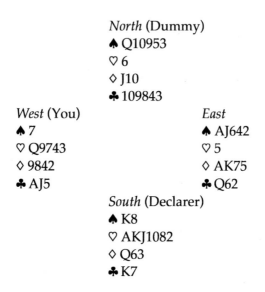

North (Dummy)
♠ Q10953
♡ 6
◊ J10
♣ 109843

West (You)
♠ 7
♡ Q9743
◊ 9842
♣ AJ5

East
♠ AJ642
♡ 5
◊ AK75
♣ Q62

South (Declarer)
♠ K8
♡ AKJ1082
◊ Q63
♣ K7

SALLY: South holds a huge hand for his 2♡ intervention—a smidgeon stronger and he would double first, then bid hearts. Players intervene on a lot less than that.

PROF: Yes, and yet South's neck is on the block for a large number. A key defensive play was for East to find the club shift at trick four instead of immediately returning a third spade. A premature spade play would permit declarer to discard a club loser, compressing a defensive club winner and the ♡9 into one trick. The properly timed defense forces declarer to ruff, exposing him to a trump promotion, because he has no more losers to discard. Remember the rhythm of this defense. E-W are best served by taking the long, patient route to their tricks.

> Junior high student
>
> Defensive timing: establish and cash side tricks, then play for trump promotion.
>
> Junior high student

SALLY: Is that because the doubler holds trump control?

PROF: Exactly—the defense can control the tempo of the defense. Incidentally, on offense E-W make at most a small partial, not a very good exchange for plus 800. When you examine a deal diagram such as this and learn the full value of your team's cards, the view is apt to be breathtaking.

19

The Tepid Doubler: Part I

SALLY: How will I know when I'm ready to graduate from my lowly status of Timid Doubler?

PROF: You will need some at-the-table successes. Until that happens, our coaching sessions can help you rehearse for a variety of situations. Take the following: you hold

♠AK654 ♡Q4 ◇K1094 ♣104

Neither vulnerable, you deal and open 1♠. LHO preempts with 3◇, partner offers a negative double. RHO passes and it's your decision.

SALLY: The same headache—do I pass for penalties or bid 3NT, trusting partner to supply stoppers in hearts and clubs? This time, there is a difference from previous problems you've posed. The trump length is sitting at my left, behind me. That's not as promising as sitting at my right, when I play after him.

PROF: Good observation. Here, trump finesses are favorable

for the declarer instead of the defender. Nevertheless, how often will declarer be able to finesse in diamonds, assuming his dummy contains entries?

SALLY: It depends upon how many diamonds dummy holds.

PROF: Dummy rates to average a singleton diamond, assuming seven diamonds with the preemptor and one apiece for the other two players. If anyone is void in diamonds, it is more apt to be RHO, not partner.

SALLY: How can you tell?

PROF: If partner were void in diamonds, he has either three spades (3-5-0-5)—yet he didn't support—or at least a six-card side suit which he didn't show. In addition, if RHO held a doubleton diamond, he would sometimes raise.

SALLY: That's subtle, but it makes sense. OK, presuming RHO holds one diamond, declarer can take only one diamond finesse. That means my ◊K remains protected.

PROF: Better still, your diamond holding with its good interiors is worth two natural tricks.

SALLY: Where is all this leading us?

PROF: We are projecting how many defensive tricks our side is worth against 3◊ doubled. Our hand suggests four tricks, and partner's approximate 10+ HCP rates to produce at least one trick, probably more. Therefore, 3◊ is a heavy favorite to go down, and all that remains is to gauge our offensive potential. What's your assessment?

SALLY: Partner could hold a full opening bid, couldn't he? In that case, 3NT looks likely, especially since I have a picture of the opposing hands.

PROF: Yes, you expect to declare to full advantage, but partner may not have enough strength to deliver game, and if he does, you should defeat 3◊ all the more. I suspect that many players would declare 3NT, simply because they are more familiar with that contract than defending 3◊ doubled.

SALLY: Count me among them.

PROF: Understandable, but look at it this way. 3NT is a chancy proposition, while defending 3◊ doubled is a surer plus, and maybe a larger one, too.

SALLY: Okay, Prof, let's try it your way.

PROF: Ultimately, we'll try it both ways. After we pass partner's negative double and LHO, the preemptor, passes, partner leads the ♠J and dummy tables:

North (Dummy)
♠ Q1092
♡ 983
◊ 2
♣ AQJ73

East (You)
♠ AK654
♡ Q4
◊ K1094
♣ 104

Dummy covers and you win the ♠K. How do you plan the defense?

SALLY: Partner holds at most a doubleton spade. Since he also appears to hold one diamond, I could try three rounds of spades. Something good may happen.

PROF: Yes, for declarer. Say he holds a doubleton spade—no law says he has to ruff. Suppose he discards a heart loser? After ruffing, partner will have to lead away from a heart combination or into dummy's ♣AQJ. If declarer needs the club finesse, he will take it and cash dummy's fourth spade for another discard while the defense sits helplessly. Remember, partner has no more trumps.

SALLY: I hadn't thought it all the way through.

PROF: That's why I stressed a defensive *plan*. Recall the general pattern for this type of defense—develop and cash side-suit winners before seeking extra trump tricks.

SALLY: All right, I'll switch to the ♡Q at trick two.

PROF: Now, we're talking. Declarer covers with the king, partner wins the ace and cashes the heart jack and ten, allowing you a club discard. Still on lead, partner produces a small spade and you win your ace. Finally, the time has come to play for a trump promotion because your side has taken its side-suit winners. By the way, what is declarer's distribution?

SALLY: Let me think. Declarer has shown two spades and has followed to three hearts. If he has seven diamonds, he has only one club.

PROF: Excellent. In theory, declarer could hold four hearts and a club void, but then partner would have led a fourth round of hearts, knowing you could overruff dummy's two of diamonds. On the actual deal, declarer's diamonds are AQ87653, leaving partner with the singleton jack. Whether declarer ruffs low, allowing partner an overruff, or ruffs with the ◇Q, your side comes to three trump tricks

SALLY: That makes the final result down four, plus 800 for us. Not that it matters, but could we have made 3NT?

PROF: Here's the full deal:

North (Dummy)
♠ Q1092
♡ 983
◇ 2
♣ AQJ73

West	*East* (You)
♠ J3	♠ AK654
♡ AJ1075	♡ Q4
◇ J	◇ K1094
♣ K9852	♣ 104

South (Declarer)
♠ 87
♡ K62
◇ AQ87653
♣ 6

Before we examine the E-W play for 3NT, verify that the defense took every trick which wasn't nailed down.

SALLY: If East plays three rounds of spades, declarer can discard a low heart. It appears that West can take no more than one heart trick.

PROF: And West might not score even that if he doesn't cash his ace immediately. Declarer, by finessing in clubs and using the

♣A and ♠Q, is in position to obtain two more discards. Declarer could escape for down two, minus 300, or down one if West slips.

SALLY: Interesting. What happens if East cashes two spades before switching to the ♡Q?

PROF: The defense loses a trick from the optimum because East can't profitably regain the lead to create the trump promotion. Retaining the ♠K preserves East's late entry.

SALLY: Looking at the diagram, I'm not sure that E-W can make 3NT.

PROF: It is touch and go, depending on the opening lead and later choices in the play. Even if nine tricks eventually materialize, who wouldn't prefer plus 800?

SALLY: I think I'm warming to your proposition.

20

The Tepid Doubler: Part II

PROF: We have progressed. A low-level penalty double is no longer an experience in a trauma center.

SALLY: Maybe not, but each time my blood pressure still rises.

PROF: Familiarity is the best medicine. To practice, let's say you hold: ♠AK932 ♡K7 ◇64 ♣AJ102. Neither vulnerable, you open 1♠, partner raises to 2♠. Since you play 1NT forcing, partner is advertising a decent raise with at least three trumps. RHO intervenes with 3♣, presenting you with a choice.

SALLY: I was going to make a game-try by bidding 3♣ myself—the rascal stole my bid. What would *double* mean?

PROF: Good question. Traditionally, the double is penalty, especially because you are sitting behind the strength. Some partnerships prefer a different treatment, but the traditional interpretation is soundly based.

SALLY: I haven't learned enough gadgets to be modern. OK, so you want me to double for penalties.

PROF: I want you keep an open mind. Start by estimating defensive tricks.

SALLY: I hope to win two spades, but partner's raise makes this uncertain. Maybe I have a heart trick, and clubs hopefully produce three tricks. Partner can't be counted on for much, perhaps one trick on average. It looks like they're going down, but maybe not enough.

PROF: Good assessment; you are making real progress. In this type of situation, I am ecstatic to hear you think in terms of tricks rather than points. Now, the next question is, what is our spade potential?

SALLY: There must be a chance for game. Partner rates to be short in clubs, leaving his HCP in helpful places.

PROF: Yes and no. I agree that partner's honors probably lie outside clubs, but it is not clear how valuable they will be. For instance, partner's hypothetical ◊KJ might sit worthlessly under RHO's A-Q. Another key factor rates to be partner's spade length. It seems that you will have to dispose of club losers, probably by ruffing. Since LHO is also short in clubs, three poor trumps in dummy will be a huge disadvantage in the play—LHO can ruff ahead of the dummy. A dummy with four trumps headed by the queen would be marvelous.

SALLY: Even assuming we think of such things, how can we possibly guess partner's spade holding?

PROF: Instead of guessing, we can consult. Suppose we double 3♣ for penalties. We have pinpointed our extra length and strength, and if partner's hand looks more suitable for offense—say a club void or extra trump length—he can head for spades. If he sits for the double, we are content. Let's assume that everyone passes our double, so we naturally lead a high spade (ace from A-K). This is what we see:

North (Dummy)
♠ J104
♡ J1032
◇ A1097
♣ 64

West (You)
♠ AK932
♡ K7
◇ 64
♣ AJ102

Partner contributes the ♠5, declarer the ♠8. Take it from here.

SALLY: In my methods, partner's lowest spade is discouraging, marking declarer with Qx. I'm not continuing spades to establish dummy's jack, but I wonder where I should shift. If partner holds the ♡A or even the queen, I might get a heart ruff.

PROF: Would that add trump tricks?

SALLY: Oh, I see. If declarer has the ♣KQ, as seems likely, and I score a ruff with my club deuce, I still take three trump tricks, just what I started with.

PROF: Exactly, and what if declarer has the ♡AQ? Your ♡K shift blows a trick and maybe a tempo. In general, when you have a sound penalty double, as here, there is no urgency about scoring ruffs. Your pretty trump interiors stand up on their own.

SALLY: Okay, let's try a diamond shift. It's less dangerous than a heart, and I might strike gold.

PROF: Yes, and there is an additional reason to play diamonds. We deduced that declarer began with ♠Q8. If allowed, he will force out your ♠K and generate a discard with dummy's ♠J. If you remove the ◇A, you strip dummy's entry to the late spade winner.

SALLY: Hadn't thought of that either; it's so frustrating.

PROF: Hang in, Sally. Declarer wins the ◇A, partner signaling encouragement, and continues by running dummy's ♡J to your king. Finish it off.

SALLY: I'd like to cash with my spade winner and exit with my last diamond.

PROF: Partner wins the diamond with his jack and returns the ◇Q; declarer ruffs with the ♣9, you overruff with the ♣10. The defensive damage has been done—your side has scored two spades, one heart, one diamond, one overruff, and two later trump tricks. Down three, plus 500. Check the full deal:

<pre>
                    North (Dummy)
                    ♠ J104
                    ♡ J1032
                    ◊ A1097
                    ♣ 64
West (You)   East
♠ AK932   ♠ 765
♡ K7   ♡ 9854
◊ 64   ◊ KQJ83
♣ AJ102   ♣ 5
                    South (Declarer)
                    ♠ Q8
                    ♡ AQ6
                    ◊ 52
                    ♣ KQ9873
</pre>

South holds a decent overcall and your partner is minimum for his raise, yet 3♣ doubled goes down three, and 4♠ your way shouldn't fetch against accurate defense. Of course, this is only relevant at IMPs. At matchpoints, whether 4♠ succeeds or not, your plus 500 is a big winner.

SALLY: I like your point about the double being flexible. Frankly, if I were East, I don't know how happy I would be leaving in the double, although I'm glad he did.

PROF: East's hand, though minimum, is within the normal range for a 2♠ call, so he should not overrule your double, especially with short spades. East's raise wouldn't appeal to strict point-counters, but he does have a singleton and a source of tricks as adequate compensation. Besides, 2♠ blocks the two-level. If East bids 1NT, South's 2♣ overcall probably emerges unscathed. Even if West doubles, East is apt to pull because he has never revealed spade support.

SALLY: I must confess that a successful penalty double is thrilling. It feels like we've pulled off a high- risk venture.

PROF: And the more we know, the less the risk.

21

The Confident Doubler: Part I

SALLY: I wonder if I've made a breakthrough. At a recent duplicate, I was dealt: ♠K73 ♡A852 ◊Q1093 ♣74. Both vulnerable, partner opened 1♣, RHO intervened 1◊, and I responded 1♡. LHO raised to 2◊ and partner made a support double (showing three-card heart support), RHO passed, and there I was.

PROF: Trembling with anticipation?

SALLY: Not exactly, but a little bell must have rung. I was wrestling with the options of crawling into a 2♡ hole or advancing to 2NT, when, suddenly, I stopped in my tracks. Could this be the spot for a penalty pass? I had those lovely interiors in trumps, and I was sitting behind the intervenor.

PROF: Did you have any special agreements about partner's support double?

SALLY: Just that it showed three-card heart support and an opening bid, any strength. It didn't sound like partner had more than a minimum since both opponents showed values. Still, I thought I had good defense; a couple of tricks in the majors and two trump winners. You've told me to play opening bidder for a minimum of two defensive tricks, so it looked like down one.

PROF: Did you take the vulnerability into account?

SALLY: Sure. They were vulnerable, meaning that a one-trick set would be worth 200 for our side. That's matchpoint gold.

PROF: Especially on a deal like this, where neither side has potential beyond a part score. Evidently, you elected the penalty pass, and I'm proud of you.

SALLY: Don't you want to know the result?

PROF: I'm sure you'll tell me, but, ultimately, it doesn't matter to me if they made 2◊ doubled. You took the percentage action, and, in the long run, you will come out far ahead.

SALLY: That's sweet.

PROF: By the way, if they were not vulnerable, your decision is more difficult. Say you manage to beat them one trick. Plus 100 may not be sufficient reward if other pairs in your direction score 110 in 2♡, or 120 in notrump. Doubling for a one trick set is risky business, appropriate only at matchpoint scoring when they are vulnerable.

SALLY: Duly noted. At any rate, I led my top club against 2◊ doubled. Was that OK?

PROF: Certainly, you led partner's suit. What did the dummy look like?

SALLY: I wrote down the entire deal.

North (Dummy)
♠ 852
♡ QJ9
◇ J64
♣ QJ102

West (Sally)   *East*
♠ K73   ♠ QJ94
♡ A852   ♡ K76
◇ Q1093   ◇ 2
♣ 74   ♣ AK653

South (Declarer)
♠ A106
♡ 1043
◇ AK875
♣ 98

My partner won the ♣K, thought things over, and shifted to the
♠Q.

PROF: Bravo, partner, for taking the long view.

SALLY: Declarer won and tried to sneak a low diamond towards dummy's jack. I must say I was ready for him. I rose, cashed
my ♠K, and continued a spade. Partner won her jack and returned
to clubs, cashing her ace and playing a third round. Of course, you
see what happened.

PROF: This promoted your second trump trick, due to your
strong intermediates. Altogether, your side won two tricks in each
suit, down three, a tidy 800. What caused you to play second hand
high on declarer's trump lead? It saved you a trump trick.

SALLY: Just instinct.

PROF: Partner's spade shift, instead of pounding away at
clubs, also saved a trick. Declarer could discard a spade on the
third club, in effect compressing two losers, a spade and a trump,
into one.

SALLY: It's what you keep saying: develop the side suits before playing for ruffs.

PROF: Yes, as long as declarer has a loser-on-loser option. Notice something else about this deal. Even if the defense slips a trick,
plus 500 should garner all the matchpoints. Your side does not

have the power to reach 3NT, and, in any event, it cannot be made against accurate defense.

SALLY: It's funny, but when I was estimating tricks, it looked like a risky double. In fact, it turned into a barbecue.

PROF: As you can see, the opponents didn't bid rashly, but partner's 13 HCP were trick heavy, and your team's defense was deadly accurate.

SALLY: I guess we can't always count on those things.

PROF: This raises a couple of collateral issues. A pair that plays sound opening bids, rather than light, is in a more secure position to double for penalties. If you play a sound opening style, be prepared to exploit this advantage.

SALLY: It's great when it works, but, as you say, you have to get used to the ride.

PROF: Exactly. When penalty doubles of low contracts no longer hold any terror for you, you are apt to benefit from another advantage—intimidation. Not the unsportsmanlike kind that bridge bullies regrettably use, but an entirely ethical advantage. If you gain the local reputation of being an active doubler, and an accurate defender, your opponents are apt to think twice before bidding aggressively.

SALLY: I imagine that must be helpful. Opponents who always apply pressure in the bidding are hard to play against.

PROF: Just so, until they lose their sense of immunity. One more issue: when a contract is doubled, it raises the stakes. Not only on the scoring table but in the intangibles. Many a declarer plays less well when doubled. Call it nerves, or whatever, but a seasoned defender has the upper hand in these contracts.

SALLY: When you experts play each other, is that true?

PROF: Not really. Then, one must be wary of tipping usable information to an unflappable declarer. However, Sally, in your games and in most games, you can acquire a practical edge by becoming a more confident and frequent doubler.

22

The Confident Doubler: Part II

SALLY: Now that I'm learning to enjoy and profit from under-game penalty doubles, shouldn't I be looking for ideal situations where I can exploit my new awareness?

PROF: How delightful—there was a time, Sally, not so long ago, when such a question would have been unimaginable. There are two situations which are ripe for penalty doubles. One is where your partner has opened 1NT; the other is when partner has pre-empted. In each case, you have a clear enough picture of partner's hand to make an accurate defensive assessment.

SALLY: I know that when an opponent intervenes over partner's preempt, my double is for penalties. Negative doubles wouldn't make any sense because partner has shown a one-suiter; why ask him to bid another?

PROF: That's the theory—in traditional preemptive strategy, the preemptor has transferred captaincy to responder.

SALLY: In other words, preemptor has told his story.

PROF: Yes, and responder can do quite well by estimating

tricks, whether for offense or, in this case, defense. Remember, where preempts are concerned, count tricks, not points. Let's begin by using a typical sequence as a model:

Partner	RHO	You
3◊	3♠	?

Vulnerability is relevant. When partner is vulnerable, you can count on him to have perhaps one defensive trick. Nonvulnerable, be prepared for less. When the opponent is vulnerable, it is more enticing to double because the rewards are greater. One more principle: *do not double the only contract you can beat.* Be content, pass and defend—you don't want to chase them into a better spot.

SALLY: Okay, let's see if I grasp the principles.

PROF: Using the sequence above, neither vulnerable, what action would you take holding ♠KJ105 ♡93 ◊A7 ♣A10862?

SALLY: It looks like a juicy double. I rate my spade holding as worth three tricks, assuming the A-Q at my right. Add two aces, maybe something from partner, and they're going down.

PROF: Too quick on the trigger, Sally. I agree that they are a favorite to be set, although if Qx of spades turns up in dummy, we lose a trump trick. The greater worry is that they might make 4♡. Recall that a classic first-seat preempt denies a four-card major on the side. Thus, they rate to hold a minimum of eight hearts, and some of our spade tricks may be ruffed away in a heart contract. Sit tight; if LHO happens to raise to 4♠, then it's time to double. Try another one, same sequence: ♠Q1097 ♡KQ62 ◊8 ♣K973?

SALLY: Here, it's harder to count defensive tricks. I guess that I'm worth two spade tricks, one or two hearts, and maybe one club. I like my singleton diamond lead, but it feels too close to double.

PROF: Good judgment. Any diamond ruff we score will be at the expense of a natural trump trick, and, for all we know, they might be about to bid 4♠. There are enough HCP outstanding for that to happen. Try another, same sequence: ♠AK94 ♡A83 ◊A92 ♣Q94.

SALLY: Interesting possibilities. I think that 9♠ is there to tempt me into doubling, but my instincts say 3NT.

PROF: I'm glad you noticed the spade spots when considering a penalty double, and I'm happier still with your 3NT conclusion. You hold "convertible values"—they are useful for both offense and defense. 3NT is a heavy favorite (+400), meaning we would need to defeat 3♠ doubled by three tricks at equal vulnerability (+500) to compensate. Here's one more problem, same sequence with both vulnerable: ♠K1094 ♡AQ63 ◊97 ♣AK6?

SALLY: Isn't this like the previous problem?

PROF: It may look similar, but the differences are noteworthy. The lack of an honor card in partner's long suit should alarm you about 3NT. If the diamond king is missing, it is probably with the 3♠ bidder, offside. The defense can usually hold up their diamond winner(s) and isolate you from the dummy. The offensive risk is too great. On the other hand, defensive prospects are bright—estimate the tricks.

SALLY: Could be two spades, two hearts, and two clubs.

PROF: Certainly could be—this is the time to double. Now, let's practice defense—what's your opening lead?

SALLY: A high club or a diamond; does it matter which?

PROF: I'd lead the ◊9. The club winners aren't disappearing, and sometimes a high club lead helps declarer establish a Q-J combination. This is the dummy:

> *North* (Dummy)
> ♠ 72
> ♡ J982
> ◊ 3
> ♣ QJ9742

West (You)
♠ K1094
♡ AQ63
◊ 97
♣ AK6

Partner plays the ◊Q and declarer wins the ace. Declarer ruffs a diamond in dummy and tries the ♣Q, partner following with the three. You have the lead—what next?

SALLY: I feel stuck. I'm afraid to continue clubs because partner's lowest club signals an odd number, here a tripleton. The majors look dangerous as well.

PROF: True, but the ♠10 should be a safe exit. You maintain your two natural trump tricks while preventing a further diamond ruff. Examine the deal if you want help in tracking the continuations.

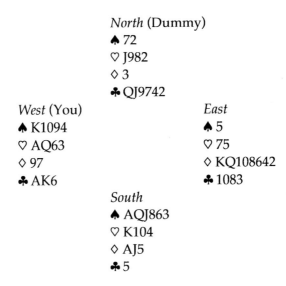

North (Dummy)
♠ 72
♡ J982
◇ 3
♣ QJ9742

West (You)
♠ K1094
♡ AQ63
◇ 97
♣ AK6

East
♠ 5
♡ 75
◇ KQ108642
♣ 1083

South
♠ AQJ863
♡ K104
◇ AJ5
♣ 5

After your ♠10 return, declarer will win cheaply and continue with ace and another trump. You cash your spade winners and have one more exit to find. By now, you have a count on declarer's distribution: six spades, presumably three diamonds due to partner's preempt, and one club, leaving a tripleton heart.

SALLY: Wait a minute. Couldn't clubs be divided 3-1 the other way, leaving declarer with a singleton heart?

PROF: That would give partner two black suit singletons, hence an unexpected four hearts. Besides, why would declarer start clubs so soon, holding nine, inviting a defensive ruff? Play declarer for three hearts and finish the defense.

SALLY: I could exit with a high club. Let declarer ruff, so what?

PROF: Not exactly. Declarer should discard his diamond loser, leaving you endplayed. Dummy's clubs are established and the ♡J

will become an entry. In effect, you would be forced to cash your
♡A, losing a heart trick. The antidote is to exit with a low heart before releasing your high club. Now the endplay is on the other
foot. If declarer wins in hand and continues hearts, you cash ♡AQ
and exit with a high club, stranding declarer with his losing diamond. If declarer wins your low heart with dummy's jack and tries
the ♣J for a throw-in, partner's ♣10 comes into play to stop the
suit, permitting you a safe club exit.

SALLY: This is a complicated deal. How many defenders in
my class would figure all that out?

PROF: Agreed, that is expert defense to produce down two
(two spades, two hearts, one diamond, and one club.) Still, ordinary defense produces down one, doubled and vulnerable, plus
200, which beats all diamond contracts (10 tricks) and three
notrump (no play). On this deal, you don't have to be a demon defender. It's enough to be a confident doubler.

23

The Confident Doubler: Part III

SALLY: Let me be sure that I have this straight. If partner's initial action is a narrowly defined bid, like a preempt or a notrump opening, that puts me in an ideal position to make a penalty double.

PROF: Yes; when you can predict your partner's strength and distribution, you can accurately gauge your side's defensive potential.

SALLY: Does the 1NT range matter?

PROF: No. Our discussion will assume 15–17. If partner is playing 12-14, you need a trick more to double, since partner supplies a trick less. But we are getting ahead of ourselves. The first decision is to come to an agreement about what *double* means in the following sequence.

Partner	RHO	You
1NT	2♡ (natural)	Dbl.

There are many ways to play double. It could be penalty, or negative, or a mirror double, saying that the opponent stole your bid, a transfer to spades. Or it could be the substitute for a natural raise to 2NT, useful if your partnership is using Lebensohl, where 2NT is artificial. Versus three-level interference, it is common to play double as negative.

SALLY: That's a lot of potential confusion. What do you suggest?

PROF: Particularly in today's hyperaggressive bidding climate, I prefer double at the two-level as penalty. A worthwhile goal is to discourage oppo-

Lebensohl was first described in the Nov./Dec. 1970 issue of *The Bridge World* by George A. W. Boehm, father of the author and the publisher. For an amusing account of the origins of the convention, refer to http://www.bridgeworld.com/default.asp?d=article_sample&f=sampleb.html.

nents from blithely intervening in your auctions. If they seldom pay a price, they will continue to interfere.

SALLY: Does it matter if their intervention is artificial?

PROF: Naturally. For example, suppose they overcall 2♣ showing an unspecified one-suiter. Many partnerships play "systems on," meaning that transfers are still available and double replaces Stayman. Personally, I like double to create a one-round force. If I double again after they reveal their suit, it is penalty and pass is forcing, inviting partner to double or bid a major. If their intervention shows two suits, double promises good defense against at least one of their suits and invites partner to double a runout.

SALLY: You really like to double for penalties, don't you?

PROF: Yes, and you may too after you become familiar with the ingredients for success. Primarily, you need defensive trump tricks. In this situation, the ideal is to hold four-card length with two of the five honors. With only one honor, look for good interiors like Q982.

SALLY: What makes four the magic number?

PROF: When you hold four trumps and partner has opened 1NT, the opponents don't have an eight-card fit in the overcalled suit, assuming partner won't open 1NT with a singleton.

SALLY: How much strength is required?

PROF: The minimum should be 7 or 8 HCP, but remember that aces and kings weigh more heavily on defense than queens and jacks. To practice, let's take an auction.

Partner	RHO	You
1NT	2♠(spades	?
	and a minor)	

Neither vulnerable, what action would you take on the four following hands?

(a) ♠KJ72   ♡A82   ◇983   ♣1075
(a) ♠KJ72   ♡10543 ◇84   ♣986
(c) ♠Q1063   ♡84   ◇QJ2   ♣QJ87
(d) ♠AJ84   ♡Q103   ◇75   ♣J1064

SALLY: (a) looks like an ideal penalty double, but (b) is a bit sketchy. Maybe if they were vulnerable I would risk it, going for the magic +200.

PROF: (a) is indeed an ideal double. On (b) it is better to pass. Your hand has promising defense against spades, but what if the opponents run to intervenor's minor? Now, your defense could be nil, and worse, you have brought partner back into the picture, encouraging him to double a runout with trump strength. **Moral: when the opponents are in the one contract you might beat, don't disturb them.**

SALLY: Good point. On (c) I like double since I think I can safely double a runout to a minor. On (d) I'm less certain. I like our prospects against 2♠ or 3♣, but what if their fit is in diamonds?

PROF: Good assessments. On (c) you are right to double 2♠, then happily double either minor at the three level. On (d) I would double 2♠, then gladly double 3♣ but pass 3◇ around to partner. You happily invite partner to double because your first double was well prepared.

SALLY: I think I've got the hang of it. At least, I am no longer spooked about doubling them in low contracts.

PROF: That's for sure. OK, you hold ♠Q1092 ♡A1063 ◇84 ♣J102.

Neither vulnerable, partner opens a 15–17 1NT and RHO intervenes
with 2◊, alerted as showing both majors. What's your plan?

SALLY: I notice you said *plan*, not *call*. I have good defense
against both of their suits. I could double now, but why let the cat
out of the bag? Couldn't I wait and double whatever suit they reach?

PROF: I'm glad to hear you have a plan, but your plan has two
flaws. First, a clever LHO looking at a major misfit might pass the artificial 2◊ with diamond length. Accepting an undoubled penalty of
50 points per trick should be a good bargain for them, not us. Second, partner might upset our headhunting plan. Suppose LHO picks
his better major and partner decides to compete in a long minor.

SALLY: I thought the 1NT opener isn't supposed to stick in his
oar, uninvited.

PROF: You're right, he isn't, but why take that chance? Partner
might well conclude that there are no bright defensive prospects
against 2♡/2♠ precisely because you *didn't* double 2◊. Indicate
penalty interest immediately by doubling and save the sequence
pass-double for something else, like a natural raise to 2NT.

SALLY: OK, I double—what happens?

PROF: LHO bids 2♡, passed around to you.

SALLY: As planned, I double.

PROF: All pass. Partner leads the ♣A (ace from A-K) and
dummy reveals:

North (Dummy)
♠ AK873
♡ KQ984
◊ 95
♣ 7

East (You)
♠ Q1092
♡ A1063
◊ 84
♣ J102

You follow low, an attitude signal when the master hand appears
in dummy (*see Chapter 15, Separating Signals, p. 78*). Partner shifts to
the ♡5, dummy plays the queen, and you win the ace. What next?

SALLY: This feels awkward because I know nothing about declarer's hand.

PROF: Well, let's see what we do know. Given partner's 1NT opening, how many hearts does declarer hold?

SALLY: Now I get it. The missing hearts must split 2-2—declarer wouldn't bid 2♡ on a singleton.

PROF: Therefore, how many spades with South?

SALLY: I see; no more than two, given the 2♡ preference.

PROF: Using these inferences, how should you defend? Bear in mind that North, dummy, holds the master hand.

SALLY: You've spoon-fed me through this—I return a low trump to stop a spade ruff.

PROF: Good. Declarer follows low and partner's jack drives out dummy's king. Declarer calls for the ♠AK, discarding a club on the second round, and continues with a low spade. Your move.

SALLY: We are going to win two spade tricks now, no matter what, since declarer is out of trumps.

PROF: Yes, but it may matter which defender wins the next trick. If you duck, partner is on lead with his ♠J and he might not have a safe continuation. It's time to check the deal:

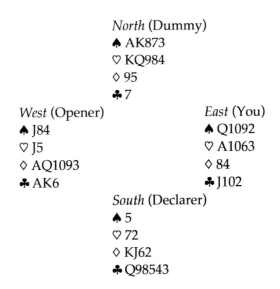

North (Dummy)
♠ AK873
♡ KQ984
◊ 95
♣ 7

West (Opener)
♠ J84
♡ J5
◊ AQ1093
♣ AK6

East (You)
♠ Q1092
♡ A1063
◊ 84
♣ J102

South (Declarer)
♠ 5
♡ 72
◊ KJ62
♣ Q98543

To maximize this defense, you should rise with the ♠Q and return the ♣J, reducing the long trump hand to your length. Declarer may as well play the fourth spade to establish his fifth. You win and shift to a diamond so that partner doesn't get endplayed, Partner cashes his diamonds and exits with a high club, pumping dummy once more. This is declarer's last trick—he never enjoys the fifth spade because you have gained trump control.

A student

When leading or shifting to trumps from a doubleton, begin with the lowest. It never hurts to save the higher trump, and that's why low-high signals a doubleton trump.

A student

SALLY: How many down?

PROF: Three; the defense wins two spades, three hearts, two diamonds, and a club. Plus 500 should be worth a lot.

SALLY: Partner made a beautiful shift at trick two.

PROF: Indeed. He could draw your inferences about declarer's probable major suit lengths, and his trump shift protected the value of your spade holding. Note that it was important for him to retain the ♡J—this allowed you to continue trumps while preserving your ten-spot. Still, even plus 300 would be very good on a part-score deal.

SALLY: The opponents didn't do anything rash.

PROF: Not at all—they just ran into a distributional ambush. Still, to capitalize, you had to pounce and double, then pick the contract clean.

24

Confidence Shaken

SALLY: It finally happened. My bubble burst and it feels like the end of the world—I doubt I'll ever double again.

PROF: Well, it sounds like the opponents made a doubled contract or two. When I was learning, it happened to me. A kindly expert offered consolation. "If they never make a doubled contract, you aren't doubling often enough."

SALLY: No doubt that was good advice, but these recent disasters were traumatic. I felt foolish in front of partner and the opponents.

PROF: It's a normal reaction and part of the learning process. If I help you discover what, if anything, went wrong, it may restore your equilibrium.

SALLY: I'll give it a try. Vulnerable against not, I picked up ♠J6 ♡A532 ◇K752 ♣972. Partner opened 1NT, 15–17, and RHO stuck in a natural 2♡ overcall. Since I had most of my HCP in aces and kings and four trumps, I doubled. It has worked for me before. Everyone passed. I thought about the lead and decided on the ♠J, hoping for a ruff.

PROF: Did you note the full deal?

SALLY: I did; it must be masochism.

PROF: On the contrary; it will help promote a cure.

SALLY: Here it is, and it's not a pretty picture.

```
                  North (Dummy)
                  ♠ A108542
                  ♡ 9
                  ◇ 93
                  ♣ QJ84
West (Sally)                       East
♠ J6                               ♠ KQ93
♡ A532                             ♡ J4
◇ K752                             ◇ Q64
♣ 972                              ♣ AK105
                  South (Declarer)
                  ♠ 7
                  ♡ KQ10876
                  ◇ AJ108
                  ♣ 63
```

Of course, you see what happened. Declarer took the ♠A and led a diamond to his jack. I won and saw that we needed to remove the trump from the board. I shifted to a club, and, sure enough, partner returned a low trump. Not that it did any good because declarer wound up taking five heart tricks, two diamonds, and a spade. Minus 470 didn't improve our standing or my disposition.

PROF: The defense was well conceived but the contract was unbeatable. Sally, your penalty double was overly aggressive for two reasons. First, you lacked interior trump quality. If you double in this situation with only one top honor, your trump spots become critical. Generally, it is important for your hand to win at least two trump tricks. If you switch your heart five for dummy's nine, your hand qualifies for a penalty double. Now, careful defense would beat the contract one: you score an eventual trump promotion on the third round of spades.

SALLY: That's really fine-tuning, but maybe I'll remember the principle. This deal should sear it into my memory.

PROF: Good, because it would be a shame **to get a bad result without learning anything.** The second reason not to double was that the opponents were not vulnerable. Close doubles are inherently risky, and when the opponents are white instead of red, your upside doesn't offset the risk. Down one doubled, plus 100, is often little different from plus 50. For instance, when your side can make nothing on offense, any plus score on defense is valuable, while if you can make 110 or more in a partial, neither plus 50 nor 100 offers adequate compensation.

SALLY: So, for all those reasons, I guess I should have passed, although I hate to pass when I know we have the balance of power.

PROF: I sympathize with that sentiment, but here, assuming a natural 2NT was unavailable, I would have meekly passed and tried to win the tournament on another deal. Besides, sometimes partner reopens with a takeout double, showing a maximum notrump with a doubleton in the overcalled suit. This double you can convert.

SALLY: Thanks for the tips. Now, I have one other tale of woe to share. Both vulnerable, I held ♠K7   ♡AJ10543   ◇KJ93   ♣4. I opened 1♡ and saw the following:

Sally	LHO	Partner	RHO
1♡	2♣	2♠	3♣
3♡	5♣	P	P
?			

Partner made a forward-going bid, and I had a full opening, so I doubled. Was that crazy?

PROF: Hardly. However, you know the opponents lack the usual HCP to attempt five of a minor. When this happens, good opponents are looking at exciting distribution. It's a warning that some of your side's high cards may not cash.

SALLY: Right on target; here's the deal:

North (Dummy)
♠ Q6
♡ Q9872
◊ 82
♣ QJ83

West	*East* (Sally)
♠ J1098532	♠ K7
♡ K6	♡ AJ10543
◊ 1074	◊ KJ93
♣ A	♣ 4

South (Declarer)
♠ A4
♡ Void
◊ AQ65
♣ K1097652

As you can see, the diamond finesse works and we took only two tricks on defense, one spade and a club, minus 750.

PROF: I suspect that you had company.

SALLY: That's true; minus 750 tied for bottom.

PROF: Ironically, sometimes it is more dangerous to double a five-level contract than a low partial because the chances of distributional volatility increase. When a good pair bids higher than expected, be wary—they may know something you don't. However, the greatest danger is to become so gun-shy that you never say *double* again.

25

Confidence Shaky

SALLY: I confess, this doubling business has me unnerved. At the club I picked up ♠83　♡Q1072　◊KQ93　♣K94. Both vulnerable, partner opened 1♠, RHO intervened with 2◊, and there I was.

PROF: So many options.

SALLY: Three calls crossed my mind; 2NT, double, and pass. I rejected 2NT because I thought it denies ♡4 and is invitational to game, an overbid. A negative double explores hearts and describes my strength, but I might not be too happy if partner bids 3♣. Pass postpones a final decision, assuming partner reopens.

PROF: A reasonable appraisal of the bridge elements. Of course, there was an emotional factor to weigh. 2NT and the negative double probably commit your team to offense—pass leaves open the dreaded possibility of defending 2◊ doubled.

SALLY: My issue in a nutshell. And so, in my current frame of mind, I chickened out and let them off the hook. I doubled, partner bid 2♡ and played it there, barely scrambling home against bad splits. The recap sheet showed all kinds of results—ours was about average. I copied down the deal to show you.

North
♠ J952
♡ AJ86
◇ 62
♣ 872

West (Sally)   *East* (Dealer)
♠ 83   ♠ AQ1074
♡ Q1072   ♡ K943
◇ KQ93   ◇ 7
♣ K94   ♣ QJ10

South
♠ K6
♡ 5
◇ AJ10854
♣ A653

It looks complicated, but how would we have done defending 2◇ doubled?

PROF: [*After a lengthy pause*] It's a very interesting deal, both from declarer's standpoint and the defense. I think it will be profitable to analyze the card play in depth because it features some important principles.

SALLY: Fine. In my seat during the auction, I take it that you would have passed 2◇, then passed again, converting partner's reopening double?

PROF: Yes. I would estimate that my hand is worth four defensive tricks, three in trumps and one outside. Counting on opener for the usual minimum of two tricks, I'd take the chance of defending 2◇ since they are vulnerable. If all goes well on defense, you are aiming at the magic of plus 200 with game far from certain. Remember, for the reopening double, partner doesn't guarantee four hearts, only diamond shortness.

SALLY: On a clear day, I think I could figure all that out. After being painfully thrown, I need to climb back on my doubling horse

PROF: That's right, and you will. Against 2◇ doubled, the lead is the ♠8, East winning the ace. East should avoid the temptation of chasing a spade ruff. If declarer started with ♠K63, a spade return is apt to compress two defensive tricks—East's natural spade and West's natural trump—into one. Since it is important to dig out tricks in the side suits, the indicated shift is to the ♣Q. Now, switch your attention to declarer's predicament in case, someday, you declare a doubled partial. Declarer knows that trumps are banked on his left. His goal is to single home his trumps, eventually reducing to no more than LHO's length.

SALLY: Is that like a trump coup?

PROF: It's the trump coup's cousin, the trump endplay, useful when the trumps are offside. Accordingly, declarer wins the club shift and plays his heart to dummy's ace, then ruffs a heart. Next, he cashes his ♠K and exits with a club. Let's say the defenders cash their two club winners and play a third heart. Declarer gladly accepts the force in this end position:

                              North (Dummy)
                              ♠ J9
                              ♡ J
                              ◊ 62
                              ♣ Void

West   *East*
♠ Void   ♠ Q107
♡ Q   ♡ 9
◊ KQ93   ◊ 7
♣ Void   ♣ Void

                              South
                              ♠ Void
                              ♡ Void
                              ◊ AJ108
                              ♣ 6

Declarer has already won five tricks. To win three more for his contract, he exits with a middle diamond. West wins and exits with his last heart. Declarer ruffs with the eight and exits with the last club. When West ruffs, he is endplayed into conceding the last two tricks.

SALLY: West has no defense against the endplay?

PROF: Not at this stage, and East is unable to obtain the lead unless declarer makes the error of playing a club in the diagram. What would happen then?

SALLY: I suppose West would discard his heart and East could overruff dummy with the trump seven. West looks like a man with two more trump tricks.

PROF: Correct. To avoid the impending endplay, East must play a role earlier in the defense. Let's retrace. After the ♣Q shift at trick two, declarer plays in the same fashion, ruffing a heart and cashing a spade. When he exits in clubs, East must use the opportunity to shift to a diamond instead of pumping away in hearts. Declarer takes a losing finesse, eventually leading to a slightly different ending:

> **A** student
>
> Don't try to defend a doubled low-level contract holding a trump void. Inability to lead a trump through declarer often leaves the trump strength endplayed.
>
> student **A**

```
                      North
                      ♠ J9
                      ♡ J
                      ◇ 6
                      ♣ Void
    West                              East
    ♠ Void                            ♠ Q107
    ♡ Q                               ♡ 9
    ◇ K93                             ◇ Void
    ♣ Void                            ♣ Void
                      South
                      ♠ Void
                      ♡ Void
                      ◇ A108
                      ♣ 6
```

Declarer has won five tricks, but here, he can win only two more. If he tries leading the last club, West must ruff with the nine-spot to shut out dummy's six-spot, then safely exit in hearts. The effect of this defense is to preserve West's original three trump winners.

SALLY: Why didn't that happen the first time?

PROF: West got clogged with trumps and couldn't get out of his own way. He needed East's help of a trump lead through declarer's strength. Add these positions to your arsenal. When trumps are stacked offside, the issue is frequently an endplay. As defender with the short trumps, when nothing else is appealing, be quick to lead a trump to protect trump-rich partner from being thrown in at the end.

26

Restoring Confidence

PROF: It seems that you're going through a confidence crisis.

SALLY: It really only happens in penalty double situations.

PROF: I hope the malaise is no wider spread, but I'd be surprised if it weren't. When a player becomes tentative in one area, the loss of confidence is apt to become general, and a tentative player is a losing player. Apart from bidding favoring the bold, a player needs to be decisive in decision making, and bridge is a game of constant decisions.

SALLY: What can I do to help myself?

PROF: Be aware of your current tendency, then consciously try to fight it off. And take heart because everybody goes through slumps. Suppose I show you a situation that I encountered; it speaks to your particular problem.

SALLY: Sure, it can't hurt.

PROF: Playing matchpoints, my nonvulnerable partner opened 1◊ and my vulnerable RHO chimed in with 1♡. I held ♠843 ♡AJ2 ◊8 ♣KJ10763—what would you do?

SALLY: I guess I'm strong enough for 2♣.

PROF: That's what I thought. LHO raises to 2♡, partner rebids 3◊, and RHO competes to 3♡. What now?

SALLY: I'm through—I barely had my first bid.

PROF: Well, that's true and we misfit partner. Still, the misfit improves our defense. How many defensive tricks are we worth?

SALLY: I'm not sure of the location of the missing heart honors. If king or queen turns up with LHO, I'll probably lose my ♡J, especially if I tip my trump holding and double.

PROF: Yes, that's all possible, but it's also pessimistic. Do you see how recent experience can color your outlook? Our singleton diamond means we stand a good chance of scoring a ruff; in fact, on a good day, two ruffs. I think a moderate estimate is to rate our hand as three defensive tricks, two and a half tricks in hearts plus a half trick in clubs. Remember, we are sitting over the stronger hand, a positive feature. If we add at least two tricks from partner—his 3◊ bid showed something extra—with the opponents vulnerable, we are talking double.

SALLY: You are also talking confidence, and you are relying on expert defense.

PROF: Up to a point. I was playing with a student whose card play can be quite undependable. This is a dissuading factor against close doubles, but I decided to chance it, partly because we needed a top. Everyone passed and I led my singleton diamond. This is what I saw:

North (Dummy)
♠ KJ952
♡ 863
◊ 105
♣ A95

West (Prof)
♠ 843
♡ AJ2
◊ 8
♣ KJ10763

Partner won the first trick with the ◊J and continued with the ◊A, declarer following. What would you discard?

SALLY: I'm glad that I can overruff the dummy on the next diamond. Maybe I should throw a low spade or an encouraging club and let nature take its course.

PROF: Before you commit, visualize five defensive tricks.

SALLY: Two in diamonds, my jack and ace of trumps, then sit and wait.

PROF: Is there a threat to the waiting plan? What about dummy's spade suit?

SALLY: Partner could easily hold a spade stopper.

PROF: He could, but what if he doesn't? If declarer holds the ♠AQ, or Ax, or even Axx, you may never score a club because dummy's spades can be established for club discards.

SALLY: I've got it! Since I have two natural trump tricks, why don't I signal for a club switch. Declarer can't use the whole spade suit until he draws trump.

PROF: Brava, Sally. Here's the deal:

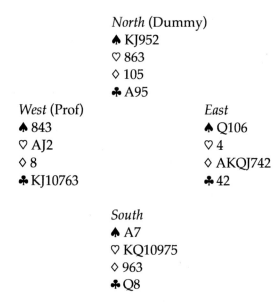

North (Dummy)
♠ KJ952
♡ 863
◊ 105
♣ A95

West (Prof)
♠ 843
♡ AJ2
◊ 8
♣ KJ10763

East
♠ Q106
♡ 4
◊ AKQJ742
♣ 42

South
♠ A7
♡ KQ10975
◊ 963
♣ Q8

When East shifts to a club at trick three, declarer is helpless. If he starts trump, we score a club in addition to our two diamonds and two hearts. It doesn't do declarer any good to ruff out partner's ♠Q on the third round because dummy lacks a re-entry—the ♣A has been dislodged. In fact, if declarer gets desperate and plays ace and another spade, finessing dummy's jack, we beat the contract two. However, down one, plus 200, scored very nicely, as it usually does. Since we rated to make 3◊ for plus 110, the double was necessary—plus 100 would have been a poor matchpoint score.

SALLY: I've noticed how matchpoint scoring encourages aggressive doubling.

PROF: When you can make a partial worth more than 100, it becomes vital to protect your equity. Back to the defense, what if partner plays a third diamond.

SALLY: Whether I overruff or not, declarer should begin to draw trumps. I can't drive out the ♣A from my side without sacrificing my ♣K. And if we never play clubs, eventually declarer can develop spades by playing A-K and a ruff, using the ♣A for reentry. His club loser goes bye-bye.

PROF: Exactly. Your level of card analysis and general experience have grown enormously. Have faith in your abilities, and don't be afraid. Go mix it up with the opponents at the club and expect to come back a winner.

27

Confidence Regained

SALLY: I want to thank you for our playing lesson at the club duplicate. I felt like you were the bridge doctor and I was the patient. I learned a lot, and I left feeling in better bridge health.

PROF: Glad to hear it. You leaped a hurdle, Sally, largely due to one notable deal where you engineered a triumph.

SALLY: I doubt the outcome would have been as pleasant if you hadn't been my partner.

PROF: I had little to do with it—you were the heroine. Let's review the deal in question to let me hear you think aloud.

SALLY: Well, I was dealt this little mitt:

♠6 ♡KQ10 ◇AKJ102 ♣KQ103

Both vulnerable, I opened 1◇, LHO put down the Stop card and bid 3♠. You passed and RHO raised to 4♠. So much for a nice, slow auction.

PROF: How did you assess your options?

SALLY: I had too much to pass. The question was whether to bid 5♣ or double. At first, I leaned towards 5♣ because at least I knew what it meant. When it comes to doubling 4♠, I never know whether it is penalty, takeout, or optional.

PROF: Strictly speaking, *all* doubles are optional—you are allowed to bid and remove a penalty double, or pass to convert a takeout double. The key is the doubler's intent. Let's apply logic to this sequence. Vulnerable opponents have preempted and raised; they rate to have a long, strong fit, reducing the usefulness of a pure penalty double. Furthermore, you are sitting under the preemptor, which diminishes the value of potential spade holdings you might hold, like KQx or AJx.

SALLY: Suppose I just have a carload of HCP. Isn't that reason to double?

PROF: Yes, provided you have distribution that is useful on offense.

SALLY: Then wouldn't this double be pure takeout?

PROF: Not exactly, because there is a pure takeout action available: 4NT.

SALLY: An unusual notrump?

PROF: Unusual in the sense that it is artificial, but here it's better to use it for three-suit takeout to bring the major into the picture. After all, with the minors, you could just bid 5♣. 4NT should depict a hand like ♠Void ♡KQJx ♢AKJxx ♣KQxx, where your offensive potential is vast. You might make a five-level contract facing a good-fitting Yarborough (no picture cards, not even a ten-spot), or slam if partner holds an ace and length in one of your suits.

SALLY: What should I do if I have a strong balanced hand, say ♠Axx ♡KJx ♢KQxx ♣KQx?

PROF: Pass. For all your HCP, you won't set them many, and sometimes they will make—the only reliable defensive tricks against wild distribution are trump tricks.

SALLY: Good point.

PROF: Furthermore, if you double with a strong notrump and partner removes with a likely spade void, your hand is poor for a five-level contract—too flat, too many losers. It is best to play that double shows a shapely hand with lots of honor tricks, but less distributional than 4NT. It is a fine line but one with great significance. 4NT releases the opponents—the defensive option is removed, which is quite a unilateral stance to take. Double is flexible, since it invites partner to exercise judgment. Most often, he will pass and try for four tricks on defense rather eleven on offense. That's just common sense. The exceptions will be hands with exciting distribution or a long fit; then he bids to make.

SALLY: Is this treatment standard?

PROF: I don't think there is one standard treatment. Bear in mind that this kind of auction, bid—raise, leaving you under the gun, is quite different from sitting over a 4♠ opening. There, you could easily hold a profitable penalty double. In general, traditional partnerships tend to play doubles of 4♠ as penalty. But in a fit auction to 4♠, double, defined as allowing for either offense or defense, is best.

SALLY: How did I come up with that call?

PROF: Good instincts.

SALLY: I'd say good luck.

PROF: In either event, I led the ◊Q and this is what dummy revealed:

North (Dummy)
♠ A104
♡ A985
◊ 73
♣ J982

         East (You)
         ♠ 6
         ♡ KQ10
         ◊ AKJ102
         ♣ KQ103

Why not relive your triumph? I know what you did, but why did you do it?

SALLY: I started thinking about your opening lead. It was natural to lead my suit, but why the queen? You didn't lead from a sequence, my ◊J told me that, so your lead was from shortness, either a singleton or doubleton diamond. That meant declarer held diamond length, five or four little ones. Diamonds was his Achilles' heel.

PROF: Excellent.

SALLY: How was declarer going to get rid of his diamond losers? By trumping, so I saw that we needed to play trumps to reduce dummy's ruffing potential. I did something very nervy—I overtook your ◊Q to shift to my spade. It wasn't an insult, was it?

PROF: Hardly; it was very well conceived. Our defensive needs were apparent to you, so it is time to take control, no matter who partner is.

SALLY: Well, I shifted to my trump, declarer won in dummy and led a second diamond. I rose, you followed, and I had to figure out the next move. Assuming declarer started with seven spades for his vulnerable preempt, you had one spade left, and it was my job to put you on play to lead it.

PROF: Exactly.

SALLY: Clubs was our only chance, so I held my breath and underled my club sequence to make sure you won the trick. Thank goodness you held the ace.

PROF: Yes. By the way, your underlead wasn't dangerous; if declarer held Ax in clubs with 7-0-4-2 distribution, we were never entitled to a club trick—dummy's ♡A provides a club discard. Here's the deal:

North (Dummy)
♠ A104
♡ A985
◊ 73
♣ J982

West (Prof)
♠ 73
♡ J6432
◊ Q4
♣ A764

East (You)
♠ 6
♡ KQ10
◊ AKJ102
♣ KQ103

South
♠ KQJ9852
♡ 7
◊ 9865
♣ 5

When I won my ♣A, I continued your defense by playing my last trump. Declarer could ruff one diamond but was stranded with a

late diamond loser. He ran his trumps, but no squeeze material-
ized because of careful discarding. Review the three-card ending:

```
                        North
                        ♠ Void
                        ♡ A9
                        ◇ Void
                        ♣ J
        West                                East
        ♠ Void                              ♠ Void
        ♡ J64                               ♡ K
        ◇ Void                              ◇ A
        ♣ Void                              ♣ K
                        South
                        ♠ 2
                        ♡ 7
                        ◇ 9
                        ♣ Void
```

You bared your ♡K to guard diamonds and clubs, I kept my
hearts. When declarer led his last trump, dummy had to discard
ahead of you—you released whatever suit dummy released.
Breathing hard, we nipped them for plus 200 and a near top. Note
that both 5♣ and 5♡ are doomed by bad splits. Defending 4♠ doubled, if we don't quickly play trumps, declarer manages to ruff two
diamonds and notches his doubled game. Once I decided not to
lead a trump, we needed all your decisions to recover.

SALLY: Going back to the bidding, why did you leave in my
double of 4♠?

PROF: I had an ace and shortness opposite your marked diamond length, both promising defensive signs. To bid, I needed
more length to withstand the likely bad splits.

SALLY: How could you be certain that my minor suit was real?

PROF: Their bidding and my spade doubleton marked you
with spade shortness. That ruled out the possibility of a convenient
diamond.

SALLY: As I said, I doubt I could have done it without you.

28
Trump Control

PROF: Pump, tap. In bridge slang, these terms mean the same thing, shortening declarer's trump by playing the forcing game.

SALLY: Bridge? They sound like dance step.

PROF: Come to think of it, there *is* a rhythm to the process. Take this hand: ♠AK65　♡KQJ82　◇9　♣Q82. As West, you open 1♡.

West	North	East	South
1♡	P	P	1♠
P	2♡	P	3◇
P	4♠	P	P
?			

First question: do you double?

SALLY: I like my chances. Declarer is headed for a bad trump split, and I have two good opening leads.

PROF: Which do you prefer?

SALLY: Does it matter much?

PROF: It's apt to make all the difference.

SALLY: Really?

PROF: If you lead your singleton diamond, you need to find partner with an entry to obtain a ruff. How likely is that, given the bidding?

SALLY: I see what you mean—partner passed 1♡. But he might have one high card.

PROF: You have time to shift to your singleton because you own the two master trumps. If a diamond ruff is available, it can wait. There is a more promising line of defense. Try to shorten declarer's trump and eventually obtain trump control by having more trumps than anyone.

SALLY: That sounds juicy.

PROF: It's defensive bliss, and, to achieve it, lead your **longest** suit, hearts. This rates to be declarer's shortest suit, and your trump entries allow you to continue the attack. You plan to tap or pump declarer repeatedly.

SALLY: OK, you talked me into the ♡K lead.

PROF: Here's the dummy:

> *North* (Dummy)
> ♠ 983
> ♡ 765
> ◊ AQ65
> ♣ A96

West (You)
♠ AK65
♡ KQJ82
◊ 9
♣ Q82

Partner produces the ♡3, declarer wins the ace. Next, declarer leads the ♠Q, you win, partner follows with the four. You continue high hearts, declarer ruffs the third round. At this point, how many trumps does declarer have?

SALLY: Let's see. He started with five; he played one round and ruffed once, leaving him with three trumps.

PROF: The same as you—it's important to keep track. Declarer now leads the ♠J.

SALLY: I win and keep pumping hearts.

PROF: Except that dummy is void in hearts. Dummy absorbs the tap with its last trump, declarer returns to his hand, draws your trumps, and claims his doubled contract.

SALLY: What went wrong?

PROF: Your rhythm was off. View the whole deal:

North (Dummy)
♠ 983
♡ 765
◊ AQ65
♣ A96

West (You)	*East*
♠ AK65	♠ 4
♡ KQJ82	♡ 943
◊ 9	◊ 10872
♣ Q82	♣ J10754

South
♠ QJ1072
♡ A10
◊ KJ43
♣ K3

To succeed, you must duck a spade, either the first or second round, so that you can win the third round as dummy plays its final trump. Now, the fourth heart forces **declarer** to take the tap. By forcing South to ruff twice, your last trump is elevated to master trump. When declarer tries to cash diamonds, you ruff and score your long heart. Three trump tricks and two hearts, down two.

SALLY: Pretty neat.

PROF: Isn't it. Notice that declarer can save a trick. As soon as he discovers the 4-1 trump split, he must abandon trumps and play diamonds. When you ruff, declarer regains control. It's an interesting battle—each side does best to pursue the forcing game.

SALLY: I wonder if I understand the underlying principle well enough to apply it correctly.

PROF: Another example. You hold: ♠A2 ♡AQJ3 ◇KQ9 ♣J1042. Neither vulnerable, LHO opens 3♠, RHO raises to 4♠. Do you act?

SALLY: I'm content to double. Partner leaves it in with all but unbalanced hands. If he bids, he'll like my dummy. If he passes, I hope we beat them.

PROF: Exactly. Partner does pass and leads the ♡2. Dummy presents:

> *North* (Dummy)
> ♠ J3
> ♡ K10
> ◇ A742
> ♣ AKQ97
>
> > *East* (You)
> > ♠ A2
> > ♡ AQJ3
> > ◇ KQ9
> > ♣ J1042

You capture dummy's king with your ace. Plan the defense.

SALLY: Presumably, declarer has seven spades. From the lead, I place declarer with three hearts, therefore three minor-suit cards. I see no hope of scoring any diamond tricks because dummy's clubs will furnish discards, if needed. Maybe partner has a spade honor...

PROF: In today's active preemptive climate, it's possible, but don't count on it.

SALLY: Well, I'm stuck. I'll just cash my second heart, exit with a high diamond, and pray.

PROF: Think about the role of trump control.

SALLY: I could play two rounds of trump, stopping a heart ruff.

PROF: That won't work against king-queen-seventh of spades. Declarer will claim six spade tricks and four minor-suit winners. Check the full deal to see if you can find the killing defense.

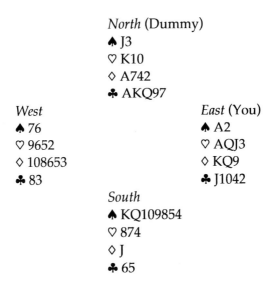

North (Dummy)
♠ J3
♡ K10
◇ A742
♣ AKQ97

West
♠ 76
♡ 9652
◇ 108653
♣ 83

East (You)
♠ A2
♡ AQJ3
◇ KQ9
♣ J1042

South
♠ KQ109854
♡ 874
◇ J
♣ 65

SALLY: I have to work out some way to get three heart tricks to go with my ♠A, but I just don't see it.

PROF: At trick two, try shifting to a low spade!

SALLY: What a strange play. However, if declarer plays a second round of trumps, I win and cash enough hearts to beat him. If declarer plays a second heart, the same thing happens. I win, cash my ace of trumps, and take the third heart. If declarer tries for a quick discard on the clubs, partner still has a trump to ruff the third round. I guess we have a counter for anything declarer does.

> **Junior high student**
>
> Many defenders automatically shift suits when declarer ruffs their lead. Unfortunately, that blind spot prevents them from enjoying a successful tap defense, bleeding declarer of trumps.
>
> Junior high student

PROF: We do, indeed. All this is made possible by retaining your trump ace, the control card. Holding that prime card, you are able to dictate the rate at which trumps are drawn. It is quite a pretty concept.

29

Going for the Kill

SALLY: I know there's more to bridge than doubling, but it sure feels great to pull off a close double. It feels even better when you have set the opponents up for the kill.

PROF: You have plenty of competitive juice, just like any successful player. I imagine you could be persuaded to describe your triumph.

SALLY: Come on, Prof. I don't get to toot my horn much, and, in the end, it wasn't much of a triumph. Our side vulnerable, I held: ♠AJ10 ♡A1092 ◊J72 ♣853. My partner opened 3◊, RHO doubled. You've taught me to plan in these situations, not just take it one bid at a time. On offense, I guessed we would usually make 3◊, either winning seven diamonds and two aces, or six diamonds plus a third major suit trick.

PROF: Agreed

SALLY: On defense, if they reached spades or clubs, I thought my hand was worth three tricks. If they played hearts, prospects were even better due to my trump stack. Since partner preempted vulnerable, I played her for a trick—our style tends to be sound.

PROF: Fair enough. Where did these assessments lead you?

SALLY: I decided we needed to protect our position of +110. To do that, I wanted to push them one level higher, then be ready to double, so I raised the ante to 4◊.

PROF: A bold, well-conceived plan.

SALLY: Thanks. My LHO doubled 4◊ (responsive—general strength, short diamonds), partner passed, and RHO started to think. Suddenly, I didn't feel too comfortable. What if RHO passed, leaving partner in 4◊ doubled? We could go down one, giving them +200, a bottom board for us.

PROF: That's the main risk in your plan, but duplicate bridge is not for the faint of heart. I like your odds because the opponents never know what tricks will cash against a preempt. That's an advantage to having long, strong trumps—it's harder for the opponents to double you.

SALLY: Well, I guess that's so because RHO finally pulled the responsive double to 4♡.

PROF: Delightful.

SALLY: That's what I thought—I doubled. Everyone passed, and I led a low diamond.

PROF: What would you have done if an opponent had run to 4♠ or 5♣?

SALLY: I was going to keep on doubling.

PROF: Good. I just wanted to make sure that you had a plan.

SALLY: Against 4♡ doubled, my diamond lead brought down this dummy:

North (Dummy)
♠ Q953
♡ QJ86
◇ Q9
♣ Q106

West (You)
♠ AJ10
♡ A1092
◇ J72
♣ 853

Partner won the ◇K and continued ace, South ruffed. Declarer plunked down the ♡K, I won, partner following, and thought things over. Declarer was already marked for four hearts and a singleton diamond. His distribution was likely to be 4-4-1-4, and he probably owned the high clubs and ♠K to bid vulnerable at the three level. Since my spade tricks looked safe, and we weren't due any club tricks, I tried the effect of a third diamond. The ruff-sluff wasn't going to hurt me, and by weakening their trump holding, I might promote a trump for myself.

PROF: High marks, Sally, for realizing that yielding a ruff-sluff won't damage the defense, as long as declarer has no losers to sluff.

SALLY: Well, I thought I was very clever, but declarer was no slouch. He sluffed a spade from dummy, ruffing in hand, and led a spade towards the queen. I ducked, declarer returned to hand in clubs to lead a trump. I'm sure he would have finessed the eight since I had doubled, so I inserted the nine, forcing dummy's jack. Was that right?

PROF: I agree that declarer would have taken a deep finesse—your penalty double alerted him to an unusual trump division.

SALLY: Declarer and I inspected the trump situation. I was sure that I was due another trump trick, holding 102 under dummy's Q8, and declarer was now void in trumps.

PROF: Appearances, though, were deceiving. I imagine the full deal closely resembled this:

North (Dummy)
♠ Q953
♡ QJ86
◊ Q9
♣ Q106

West (You)
♠ AJ10
♡ A1092
◊ J72
♣ 853

East
♠ 84
♡ 3
◊ AK108643
♣ 972

South
♠ K962
♡ K754
◊ 5
♣ AKJ4

Declarer can concede two spades, then cash his clubs, arranging to lead from his hand at trick 12. You are caught in a trump coup, forced to ruff ahead of dummy. Alternatively, declarer could strip your clubs and toss you in with a spade. Eventually, you must break trumps, providing the same proven finesse. Either line lets declarer escape for down one.

SALLY: Plus 100 wasn't much of a score since 3◊ makes +110. I have a nagging feeling that I could have defended better.

PROF: I'll explain how, but you should take considerable credit for your performance on this deal. In the bidding, you counted tricks, not points, which is the only way to reach valid conclusions facing a preempt. You followed with a courageous double. If something goes wrong, you wind up with a poor result—that's why it requires courage.

SALLY: Thanks for the compliments, but now that I study the deal, I notice that we're cold for 3NT. Should I have bid it?

PROF: Monday morning quarterbacking. Aside from the hypothetical possibility of losing the first five club tricks, you have no assurance that the diamonds will run—partner could have preempted on king-queen-seventh or ace-queen-seventh. If the opponents stop diamonds, 3NT is set a bundle, vulnerable. But there is a defensive idea worth noting. **When you hold four trumps to the ace, be reluctant to release your ace.** We know that the trump ace represents control; retaining it is often an advantage. Review the play: at trick three, declarer offers you a tempting ♡K. Resist it. Let's say declarer continues a second trump—you duck again, keeping control. Declarer plays as he did, coming to hand with a club to start spades, which you properly ducked. Declarer cashes two more clubs, reaching this ending:

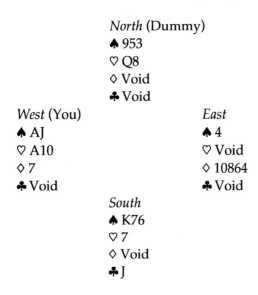

North (Dummy)
♠ 953
♡ Q8
♢ Void
♣ Void

West (You)
♠ AJ
♡ A10
♢ 7
♣ Void

East
♠ 4
♡ Void
♢ 10864
♣ Void

South
♠ K76
♡ 7
♢ Void
♣ J

Note an alteration from your early defense—I have had you unblock your ♢J on the second trick, preserving the threat of running partner's diamonds if you gain trump control. Let's say that declarer, having lost one trick, leads a spade. You win cheaply, cash the trump ace, and force dummy with a diamond, promoting the ♡10 for down two, doubled, +300. If declarer leads a trump, you win, tap dummy with a diamond, and wait for two spade tricks, again down two. In the most interesting variation, declarer leads the 13th club. To take four defensive tricks in this position, you must ruff low. If dummy discards, you cash the ♡A, exit in diamonds, and wait for two spades. If dummy overruffs and tries to endplay you in trumps, you can safely exit with your preserved low diamond—East takes the rest of the tricks.

SALLY: Fancy footwork, Prof.

30

Partnering a Demon Doubler

PROF: Sally, you are approaching the status of Demon Doubler, that feared opponent who knows how to wield the double card in the bidding box. The card is a demonic red.

SALLY: Come on, Prof; you give me too much credit.

PROF: I've tracked your progress, and I can see that you're on the threshold. Now, a new issue arises—what if you find yourself partnered by a fellow demon doubler?

SALLY: Like whom?

PROF: Like me. You may face certain bidding problems you've rarely encountered. For instance, what do you make of the following sequence?

Partner	RHO	You	LHO
1♡	2◇	P	P
Dbl.	P	2♠	P
3♣			

SALLY: Partner makes a normal reopening double, I take out to spades, and partner bids clubs. What's so unusual?

PROF: Why doesn't partner bid 3♣ immediately, instead of doubling?

SALLY: Does his chosen sequence show extra strength?

PROF: In both cases, partner's advance to the three level shows extras because you have not confirmed strength or fit. So, the question remains: What's the difference between the direct 3♣, and the delayed?

SALLY: I'm stumped.

PROF: The reason partner doubles before bidding clubs is to enable you to pass for penalties. Playing negative doubles, your first-round pass is ambiguous. Either you pass because you have a weak holding, or you hold a decent hand with long, strong diamonds, a trap pass. Opener caters to the trap pass possibility by doubling, expecting you to pull with weakness.

SALLY: That sounds classic.

PROF: It's an adjunct to negative doubles. The only times opener makes some bid other than double is when he has no interest in defending. Connecting the dots, partner was prepared to defend 2◇ doubled, yet he didn't pass 2♠. His likely distribution is 2-5-1-5, perhaps a hand like: ♠Kx ♡AKxxx ◇x ♣AQ10xx. With 3-5-1-4, partner would have passed 2♠. With a diamond void, he should be reluctant to double. Remember why a trump void makes this type of defense awkward?

SALLY: The defense may need to push a trump through declarer to protect partner from a trump endplay. (*See Chapter 25, Confidence Shaky, p. 129.*)

PROF: Exactly. Furthermore, if partner were 1-5-2-5 or 1-6-1-5, he should reopen 3♣, bypassing double, since he is totally unprepared for spades. What if responder jumps to 3♠, anticipating a spade fit, holding: ♠J10xxxx ♡xx ◇Axx ♣xx? The partnership is out on a brittle limb. Partner's actual sequence implies a tolerance for spades—say a doubleton honor—so you could rebid spades if you misfit clubs.

SALLY: That's a lot of inferences; do you think I'm ready?

PROF: Your goal is to graduate to Demon Doubler, so you must be prepared to partner a member of the Order. Let's take another type of problem you will eventually encounter. Neither vulnerable, playing matchpoints, you hold ♠1074   ♡AQ873   ◊74   ♣J84. The bidding develops:

LHO	Partner	RHO	You
1◊	1♠	2◊	2♠
3◊	Dbl.	P	?

SALLY: Both partner and I have bid, so I interpret his double as penalty and I pass. It can't be that simple—what am I missing?

PROF: Think about everyone's diamond length.

SALLY: Well, that's a good point. The opponents usually have nine trumps when they compete to the three level.

PROF: Especially in today's total-tricks environment.

SALLY: That leaves partner with a doubleton diamond, so why did he double?

PROF: He doubled to show extra values and a hand of mixed orientation to defend or play spades, a hand with two-way strength. This is an effective treatment against bid-and-raise auctions.

SALLY: It's no longer a pure penalty double?

PROF: No, it's cooperative, asking partner to use good judgment.

SALLY: Okay, but how do I decide when to pass, and when to pull?

PROF: If your hand is very flat, or you have defensive tricks in their trump suit, you sit for the double. If your hand is distributional, without defensive tricks, you pull. How do you grade this hand?

SALLY: It seems to contain more offense than defense, although I like that heart A-Q combination, a trick and a half.

PROF: Good observation, thinking tricks rather than points, but the downside is that your defensive strength is located in a long suit, reducing its weight.

SALLY: Is there is an increased chance that one opponent will have heart shortness?

PROF: Yes. On balance, this is a better hand to pull than pass. Here's a hand to pass the double: ♠xxx   ♡AJxx   ◊xx   ♣QJ10x.

It's flat and contains about two defensive tricks, above average for a simple raise to 2♠.

SALLY: Okay, on your problem hand, I'll pull to 3♠.

PROF: Don't stop thinking too soon. I agree it seems best to bid, but consider your options.

SALLY: That's interesting. Are you suggesting that I try 3♡?

PROF: Why not? It adds a dimension to your description; minimal spades with a decent heart suit. This opens the gates to other possibilities. Put yourself in partner's position, holding: ♠AKQJ3 ♡K52 ◇85 ♣K75. How should he react?

SALLY: I guess his hand grows in value—that ♡K becomes a pretty big card.

PROF: Indeed. Anticipating the double fit, and promoting the position of his other king, behind the opening bidder, partner is poised to jump to 4♠. Here is the deal:

North (You)
♠ 1074
♡ AQ873
◇ 74
♣ J84

West
♠ 865
♡ J106
◇ QJ93
♣ Q92

East (Dealer)
♠ 92
♡ 94
◇ AK1062
♣ A1063

South
♠ AKQJ3
♡ K52
◇ 85
♣ K75

How will 4♠ fare, compared with 3◇ doubled?

SALLY: 4♠ looks good to me, and 3◇ doubled is probably down only one.

PROF: Right. In 4♠, East might overtake in diamonds and underlead his ♣A—are you ready for that?

SALLY: Yep. I play him for the points, rise with my king, draw trumps, and run hearts, making an overtrick.

PROF: Exactly. In 3◊ doubled, East should play you for the missing strength and eventually lead towards the ♣Q, holding his club losers to one. Your plus 100 would score poorly. Still, South's cooperative double is a good move since there are layouts where 3◊ goes down two tricks, while all your side can make is a partial. South has too much defensive potential to release the opposition, and not enough shape to commit to offense. Double is his ideal straddle position, provided that partner knows how to exercise judgment.

SALLY: I don't know if I can promise that yet.

PROF: Let's keep practicing. Neither vulnerable, matchpoint scoring, you pick up: ♠5 ♡KJ93 ◊QJ982 ♣K102. Here's the auction (you are West):

East	South	West	North
1♣	1♠	Dbl.	3♠ (Preempt)
P	P	?	

SALLY: I desperately want to act. If I bid 4◊, it seems like a shot in the dark. I guess double does the trick. It's still takeout, right?

PROF: Yes, it describes a negative double with extra high-card values; partner is invited to use his judgment. Partner judges to pass, making the contract 3♠ doubled. What's your lead?

SALLY: Partner must have some spade strength, probably fewer than four hearts. The ◊Q looks normal.

PROF: Perhaps it is against 3♠ undoubled, but here a trump lead is indicated.

SALLY: Why? I think of a singleton trump as a lousy lead.

PROF: Not against a doubled partial. Consider this: your side has the balance of power, with length and strength in all the side suits. The only suit declarer can use for extra tricks is the trump suit, and the 3♠ preemptive raise typically delivers side-suit short-ness. A trump lead and continuation are necessary. Consult the deal diagram:

North (Dummy)
♠ Q962
♡ 8762
◊ A1053
♣ 7

West (You)
♠ 5
♡ KJ93
◊ QJ982
♣ K102

East
♠ KJ3
♡ Q4
◊ K74
♣ AJ863

South
♠ A10874
♡ A105
◊ 6
♣ Q954

If you lead the ◊Q, dummy wins and plays a club. Even if partner ducks the ♣A, allowing you to win and shift to a trump, it is too late. Declarer pursues a merry crossruff, scoring three club ruffs in dummy, four trump tricks in hand, and two aces, making 3♠ doubled. If you find the trump lead, partner will win the first round of clubs to continue king and another spade. This defense holds declarer to one club ruff, defeating 3♠ doubled two tricks—quite a difference.

SALLY: I see the effectiveness, but I worry about finessing partner's spade holding.

PROF: That must take a back seat when your side's trump holding is sandwiched. The defenders aren't proposing to win lots of trump tricks, as when the doubler holds a trump stack behind the bidder. Here, the goal is to reduce declarer's ruffing power. By the way, notice that 3NT E-W is down two against the normal spade lead. Plus 300 in 3♠ doubled is a truly gratifying result.

SALLY: Doubling a bid–raise sequence has a dynamic of its own.

31

Sally Fourth, Demon Doubler

PROF: I was really gratified with our recent duplicate session. You've come of age, Sally. I feel very proud of you, and I hope you are happy with your growth.

SALLY: I am, and I thank you for it.

PROF: I didn't have that much to do with it. To do my job well, I try to be a catalyst. I provide tools and encouragement, hoping to promote a chemical reaction. You are the one who goes home, does the work, and builds yourself into a player.

SALLY: I think you're underbidding, but we'll let it pass.

PROF: In our session of many good results, there was one deal that was especially pleasing.

SALLY: I know which one you mean, but I don't have total recall of the details.

PROF: You held: ♠J10843 ♡K4 ♢A9843 ♣K. Matchpoints, neither vulnerable, I opened 1♣, your RHO intervened with 1♠, and you faced the first of many decisions.

SALLY: I passed, trapping, hoping for a penalty. I used to bid

2◊, aiming at 3NT, but I've now come to enjoy collecting numbers.

PROF: You passed in tempo—that's important to avoid revealing information. After your LHO passed, I guessed to reopen with a double, holding ♠AQ ♡AQ108 ◊65 ♣Q10942. I couldn't tell whether you had made a trap pass or a weakness pass. If it was the latter, reopening might be very wrong. From my perspective, we have no safety in a diamond contract, or the opponents might pull themselves together and bid a laydown game.

SALLY: I'm glad you doubled, giving me the chance to spring my trap and pass.

PROF: South decided to escape from 1♠ doubled into 1NT. This was passed around to you for the next decision.

Prof (West)	North	East (You)	South
1♣	1♠	P	P
Dbl.	P	P	1NT
P	P	?	

SALLY: I wasn't sure what to do, but I knew I must do something—we had the balance of power. I toyed with bidding 2◊ or even 3NT, but then I came to my senses. How could they possibly take tricks in 1NT? We had the points and their only long suit, North's spades, was never going to run. I began to wonder why South didn't bid 1NT the first time, and I concluded that he must be pretty weak. So I doubled again.

PROF: Actually, this was your first double, but your penalty pass the previous round *felt* like a penalty double. You judged very well. The opponents were on the run, and if we had the power to make 3NT, plus 400, those same nine tricks would leave South down three doubled, plus 500.

SALLY: Everyone passed 1NT doubled, leaving you on opening lead. You made a great choice, the ♠A. How did you figure that?

PROF: Opening leads are an extension of the auction. Your penalty pass of 1♠ promised spade length and strength, so my powerful spade doubleton indicated that spades was our best suit.

SALLY: Isn't that ironic. They bid only one suit, and the logic of the bidding reveals that suit to be their weak link.

PROF: Fascinating, isn't it? Here's the complete deal:

North (Dummy)
♠ K9762
♡ J73
◇ KQ
♣ 763

West (Prof.)
♠ AQ
♡ AQ108
◇ 65
♣ Q10942

East (You)
♠ J10853
♡ K4
◇ A9843
♣ K

South
♠ 4
♡ 9652
◇ J1072
♣ AJ85

At trick two I continued the ♠Q, South ducking and shedding a heart. Next, I shifted to a low club.

SALLY: That worked wonders, but wasn't it a bit dangerous?

PROF: It was quite likely that your hand contained a club honor—even the jack would do—since you were known to have relatively few HCP in the major suits.

SALLY: Okay, that makes sense. I remember that declarer allowed my ♣K to hold.

PROF: He was trying to retain the only entry to his hand, hoping to establish diamonds.

SALLY: I continued the ♠J to establish another spade trick.

PROF: Good move. I discarded the ◇5 to discourage diamonds. Dummy's ♠K won and declarer led a diamond honor. You won your ace, cashed the ♠10, and shifted to the ♡K. We took four heart tricks, completing a run where we scored nine of the first ten tricks. In the three-card ending, declarer reduced to the winning combination of ◇J10 and ♣A, having unblocked dummy's remaining diamond honor on our fourth heart. That was a clever move, but we collected down three, plus 500, a top.

SALLY: Could declarer have done better if he had won the second spade and started diamonds?

PROF: Not necessarily. Win your ace immediately while the diamonds are still blocked. As long as we play a club before running hearts, declarer's communications remain tangled. If declarer releases his ♣A, he loses the entry to his diamonds. If he ducks, you cash spades, then run hearts. Although this permits dummy's unblocking diamond discard, the defense comes to three spades, four hearts, one diamond and one club, essentially the same nine tricks we did take.

SALLY: I'm glad we—or rather I—didn't slip on defense, because we can make 3NT, and plus 300 wouldn't have been enough.

PROF: True. Now, if we had been playing IMPs, your bidding decisions would be easier because less depends on waging a pinpoint defense. If we finish plus 300, we might lose a modest three IMPs against 3NT made at the other table; plus 500 rates to win three. At IMPs, it's always better to take the bird-in-hand, a sure, sizable plus on defense, rather than aim at a speculative game on offense. Here, at matchpoints, with so much riding on every trick, your decisions took guts and skill.

SALLY: Well, having a fine partner adds confidence.

PROF: This whole business of employing penalty doubles rests on partnership confidence. Not only is tight defense often required, but sometimes collaboration in the auction is needed to set opponents up for the kill.

SALLY: There is an awful lot of trust involved.

PROF: Yes; trust of partner, trust of principles. But that is bridge at its best, a partnership game.

SALLY: Doubling a final contract raises the bet, in effect, and adds to the pressure.

PROF: Quite so, but the extra pressure is also felt by declarer. No question, an aggressive penalty double posture is not for the faint-hearted. However, neither is competitive tournament bridge.

SALLY: And I have learned that success in this area sure helps make you a winner.

Doubling Two-Suited Bids

When an opponent intervenes with an Unusual Notrump, Michaels Cuebid, Cappelletti, or any other convention that shows two suits with one bid, double should be used to express penalty interest; a decent four-card holding in their prospective trump suit and the balance of power. For example, if South bids 1♡ and West intervenes with 2♡ (Michaels–spades plus an undisclosed minor), North should double holding: ♠Q1052 ♡93 ◊AJ732 ♣K8.

The goal is to alert South that there is blood in the water. North is ready and eager to double a runout to 2♠ or 3◊, and South is invited to double 3♣ with trump length and strength. South should avoid bidding ahead of North when willing to defend a doubled partial.

32

Final Exam

In the first five questions, one auction is given with two different hands that you might hold. Decide your call for (a) and (b). Assume equal vulnerability. (*Answers are on p. 171.*)

1.   1♠   P (You)   4♠   Dbl
        P   ?

    (a) ♠53   ♡Q97542   ◊K983   ♣7

    (b) ♠64   ♡A10863   ◊J102   ♣K83

2. 1♡ (You)   2♣   P   P
    ?

(a) ♠J87   ♡KQJ65   ◊AK4   ♣104

(b) ♠5   ♡AQ10942 ◊A83   ♣KQ6

3. 1NT (15-17)   2♠   ?(You)

(a) ♠AKJ   ♡J2   ◊Q9852   ♣983

(b) ♠J1053   ♡K863   ◊KJ4   ♣75

4. 3♡   Dbl.   P   ? (You)

(a) ♠8   ♡A862   ◊K1052   ♣Q876

(b) ♠K73   ♡KQ5   ◊74   ♣K9532

5. 2♡ (weak)   P (You)   3♡   P
    P   ?

(a) ♠J1083   ♡5   ◊Q862   ♣AQ92

(b) ♠4   ♡QJ103   ◊K954   ♣AK104

6. You hold: ♠3 ♡AJ104 ◊J7 ♣1086532. The auction:

2♡ (weak)   P (You)   4♡   P
P   ?

(a) What's your call?

(b) What's your lead?

7.   You hold: ♠AK984   ♡AQ6   ◇K1092   ♣4. Equal vulnerability:

1♠ (You)   3♣ (Preempt)   P   P
?

(a) What's your call?

(b) Let's say you double, and everyone else passes. Partner leads the ♠7, and this is what you see:

> *North* (Dummy)
> ♠ QJ102
> ♡ K98752
> ◇ 8
> ♣ 95
>
> > *East* (You)
> > ♠ AK984
> > ♡ AQ6
> > ◇ K1092
> > ♣ 4

Dummy covers, you win the king. Plan the defense.

8.   *Extra Credit.* You hold: ♠9863   ♡87542   ◇Void   ♣6532, neither vulnerable. The auction:

RHO	You	LHO	Partner
3◇	P	3NT	Dbl.
P	?		

It's hard to imagine being faced with a decision when you are dealt a Yarborough, but here you are. What's your call?

ANSWERS

1a. 5♡. Partner's double of a big fit auction shows a strong three-suiter, short in their suit. Your hand is clearly better suited to offense than defense because of the heart length, the likely second fit in diamonds, and slender high cards. When you bid in this situation, you are bidding to make. Sometimes, 5♡ will allow partner to bid an excellent slam.

1b. Pass. In contrast, this hand is less distributional and contains high cards that rate to produce defensive tricks. In the long run, defending 4♠ doubled is apt to yield a surer plus than bidding 5♡.

2a. Double—takeout, not promising extra strength, short in their suit, support or tolerance for the unbid suits. You will be delighted if partner converts to penalties, signifying a trap pass. If partner was not trapping, he will bid and your side will contest the partial.

2b. 2♡. Your club length and strength makes it virtually impossible that partner is trapping. Double, therefore, is futile, and, worse, it invites partner to bid spades.

3a. 3NT. Despite your spade honors, you have no unpleasant surprise for the 2♠ bidder. He knew he was missing the spade tops when he intervened; a sound opponent holds compensating strength elsewhere. Expect to make 3NT and score more points than penalizing 2♠.

3b. Double. Here, 3NT is apt to be out of reach, and the penalty against 2♠ is virtually certain. The 2♠ bidder is about to face two unpleasant surprises—he lacks an eight-card spade fit (partner has at least a doubleton for the 1NT opening), and the trumps are not dividing evenly.

4a. Pass. Your hand represents about three defensive tricks, combining high cards and ruffing value. Partner is advertising better than an opening hand to double at the three-level—estimate three defensive tricks. Expect to defeat 3♡ at least a couple of tricks, with no game certain your way.

5a & b. These two problems highlight the need for a partnership agreement. The key question: What is the meaning of a delayed double after an opposing preempt? Is it for takeout, a light balancing action, weaker than a direct double of 2♡ (5a)? Or is it a penalty double (5b)? The Professor prefers the penalty double interpretation because of the positional element. When the defensive trump strength is sitting behind, or over, the preempt, conditions are ripe for a large penalty. Balancing successfully at the three-level aims at a less certain target.

6a. Pass. Outside of the trump suit, where else will you get tricks? Partner hasn't promised a thing.

6b. A low club. Holding long , strong trumps, playing for a spade ruff should be secondary to trying to gain trump control. Opening leader's long suit rates to be declarer's short suit, or tap suit. There is plenty of time to shift to the singleton spade, if circumstances warrant.

7a. Double. Caters nicely to a penalty pass from partner (made more likely by shortness in the opponent's suit), or takeout, your primary intent.

7b. Shift to a trump. A spade ruff takes a back seat to attacking dummy's ruffing potential in diamonds. Partner's penalty pass means that declarer won't be able to draw trumps immediately. The defense should establish outside tricks, then try for a ruff or trump promotion in these doubled partials. Time is on the defenders' side when they hold trump entries. A rush to try three rounds of spades allows declarer to discard a red-suit loser while partner trumps, usually compressing defensive tricks.

8. *Extra Credit.* 4♡. Treat partner's double as takeout of the bid suit (diamonds), rather than a penalty double of 3NT. The analogy is 1♡—P—1NT—Dbl., where double is a takeout of hearts. Partner has considerable strength for his high-level entry, and your Yarborough will fit nicely and defend badly. It is a bad idea to cuebid 4◇, asking partner to pick the suit, because partner may pick a suit at the slam level, thinking you have something. By the way, 3NT may be a bluff bid with a diamond fit—there are enough HCP outstanding for partner to hold a gigantic hand. You might make 4♡, or it may turn out to be a worthwhile sacrifice. The main point is to identify and honor partner's intent (takeout).